Fairtrade Impacts

Praise for this book

'This book is a welcome addition to the growing empirical literature on the real impact of Fairtrade on rural producers, traders and farm workers in different agro-food sectors. Valerie Nelson did a remarkable job in bringing together perspectives on social justice, gender empowerment, environment and civic organization that enable a balanced appraisal of the ongoing efforts towards the renewal of Fairtrade.'

Professor Ruerd Ruben, Coordinator Food Security, Value Chains & Impact Analysis
Agricultural Economics Institute (LEI) Wageningen University and Research Centre

'This book avoids the elusive quest for attribution of impact to a non-existent generic "fair trade". It argues instead for a balance between rigour and usefulness in impact studies, showing the way forward with resourceful and instructive country case-studies about context-specific impact processes.'

Dr. Johan Bastiaensen, professor in development studies, Institute of Development
Policy and Management (IOB), University of Antwerp, Belgium

Fairtrade Impacts
Lessons from around the world

Edited by Valerie Nelson

PRACTICAL ACTION
Publishing

Practical Action Publishing Ltd
The Schumacher Centre,
Bourton on Dunsmore, Rugby,
Warwickshire, CV23 9QZ, UK
www.practicalactionpublishing.org

A catalogue record for this book is available from the British Library.

A catalogue record for this book has been requested from the Library of Congress.

ISBN 978-1-85339-906-0 Hardback
ISBN 978-1-85339-907-7 Paperback
ISBN 978-1-78044-906-7 Library PDF
ISBN 978-1-78044-907-4 eBook

Citation: Nelson, V. (ed.) (2017) *Fairtrade Impacts: Lessons from around the world* Rugby, UK: Practical Action Publishing <http://dx.doi.org/10.3362/9781780449067>

Since 1974, Practical Action Publishing has published and disseminated books and information in support of international development work throughout the world. Practical Action Publishing is a trading name of Practical Action Publishing Ltd (Company Reg. No. 1159018), the wholly owned publishing company of Practical Action. Practical Action Publishing trades only in support of its parent charity objectives and any profits are covenanted back to Practical Action (Charity Reg. No. 247257, Group VAT Registration No. 880 9924 76).

Cover photo: Tea picker, Kenya. Credit: Shared Interest. License Creative Commons, CC-BY-2.0

Printed in the United Kingdom by
Hobbs the Printers Ltd, Hampshire SO40 3WX

MIX
Paper from
responsible sources
FSC
www.fsc.org   FSC® C020438

Contents

http://dx.doi.org/10.3362/9781780449067.000

About the editor

Valerie Nelson is Principal Scientist, Social Development Specialist and Reader in International Development at the Natural Resources Institute (NRI), University of Greenwich, UK. She leads the Equitable Trade and Responsible Business Programme at the NRI.

CHAPTER 1
Introduction: the impact of Fairtrade

Valerie Nelson

Abstract

*This chapter introduces the concept of the Fairtrade movement as well as an intro-
duction to the chapters that follow. It asks whether or not Fairtrade can revise its
methods, addressing issues such as share of value and assurance to buyers. Each
chapter ultimately concludes that it is important for Fairtrade to adapt to a more
flexible approach and understand its limitations better; otherwise it is at risk of falling behind and giving way to new strategies of international companies.*

Keywords: Fairtrade, expansion, cultural economy, conventional trade,
decentralization, strategy revision

The fair trade movement combines the efforts of many different organizations with a shared aim of achieving more equitable trading partnerships
between disadvantaged producers and mostly Western consumers. This book
focuses on one strand of this movement commonly known as 'Fairtrade' – the
product certification system operated by Fairtrade International. Fairtrade has
expanded rapidly in recent years, particularly in certain products such as tea
and cocoa, but there is still a way to go before sector coverage is achieved in
many commodities. Recent developments, such as the decision by one major
chocolate manufacturer to promote their own brand rather than Fairtrade,
albeit continuing an informal collaboration with them, means that the position of Fairtrade is also not secured in international markets. Fairtrade is a
pioneer amongst the voluntary sustainability standards with a consumer
label and particularly high visibility in certain markets. Unsurprisingly it has
attracted more attention than other market-based mechanisms, including
other voluntary sustainability standards to date, although this is now beginning to change.

This collection of chapters emerges at a critical juncture for Fairtrade. Its
market expansion has been accompanied by increased attention to its effectiveness and there is increased questioning of its impact and relevance in
many quarters. The case studies and overview chapter on impact assessment
draw on detailed empirical studies of Fairtrade around the world and practical experience of conducting impact studies. The case studies highlight the
context specificity of Fairtrade outcomes and impacts, suggesting that broad
generalizations about Fairtrade effectiveness are unwise. What is needed is

http://dx.doi.org/10.3362/9781780449067.001

in-depth understanding of the complex interplay of multi-scale factors which shape livelihoods and environmental change at the local level, and of the role that Fairtrade plays in this dynamic over a period of time.

The chapter authors cast a critical eye over the key factors and processes in each place which influence the implementation and uptake of Fairtrade by producer organizations and companies and the eventual outcomes. The overview raises questions about how best to understand the outcomes and impacts of Fairtrade in a way which minimizes bias and supports rigour, but which also pays attention to usefulness and learning. Taken collectively, these chapters ask pertinent questions about the efficacy of Fairtrade and also provide practical suggestions given as to how improvements might be achieved.

Chapter 1 by Nelson and Martin situates the current (often polarized) debate on the impact of Fairtrade in the wider evaluation context. Approaches to monitoring and evaluation have emerged over past decades within international development, but appropriate approaches are contested. Mixed method approaches are highly valued, but have resource and skill implications and are not always that feasible in complex situations. Theory-based evaluation has come to the fore as a way of closely tracking and evaluating the contribution of a project or initiative against its intended theory of change, relying upon a different approach to causality. The politics of 'evidence-informed' policymaking require closer attention in international development than has been the case to date, and this includes in relation to Fairtrade. For example, even where there may be strong evidence, this evidence is not always used and can be ignored by decision-makers. In what is being called 'the post-truth' era it is not always easy to reconcile the push for evidence with the decision-making of governments or companies.

Fairtrade and other sustainability standards with limited resources face major challenges in responding to the evidence agenda. Many of the independent studies they have commissioned are criticized for not being sufficiently rigorous by those who hold to a very narrow idea of the gold standard. The Nelson and Martin chapter questions what is appropriate for Fairtrade in this context. Fairtrade, and the other sustainability standards, are already improving their own monitoring and evaluation systems, with support from their membership body ISEAL, but they continue to grapple with issues of rigour, cost, learning and utility.

Beyond the practical challenges of evaluation there are also strategic challenges. Many of the more rigorous impact evaluations funded by donors are showing mixed results. There are different reasons for this. One reason is that some impacts may not be visible as statistically visible differences, because of the high degree of variability, and the limited scale and coverage of impact assessments compared to the overall standard system implementation (many different countries and commodities) and the 'spillover' influence of Fairtrade on local markets. However, these findings also present growing questions about the capacity of Fairtrade to bring benefits to producers and its ability to tackle poverty in a transformative way, particularly in the light of the challenges facing global agriculture. Fairtrade needs to learn from evaluation work not only in a limited instrumental sense in specific localities, but to challenge the assumptions that it holds within its theory of change in order to scale up and deepen its impact.

The chapter authors in this book seek to inform debates about fair trade more widely, as well as the specific role of Fairtrade and its effectiveness, shining a light on the specifics of place and teasing out the varied strengths and weaknesses of attempts at fairer trading relations in agricultural commodities.

In the first of four case studies, McEwan, Hughes, Bek and Rosenberg provide a fascinating analysis of the cultural economy of Fairtrade raisins produced by smallholders in the Ekseteenskuil Agricultural Cooperative, South Africa. The raisins are supplied to the alternative trade organization Traidcraft plc in the UK. Following an emerging strand of fair and ethical trade critical thinking, the authors explore how Fairtrade co-produces outcomes in a particular place in interaction with local geography, history and institutions. The Ekseteenskuil farmers live in an area favourable to seedless grape and high-quality raisin production, but are highly disadvantaged by the legacies of apartheid, spatial marginality and increasing environmental risks. The communities are more riven with disputes, than they are drawn together by a sense of collective enterprise, affecting the cooperative's functioning and the effective use of the Fairtrade premium as well as being somewhat at odds with the Fairtrade conception of community. Fairtrade has delivered more stable markets, but the organization and its members face significant challenges. To build up legitimacy amongst their membership, the cooperative needs to decentralize, build upon informal inter-group networks, and improve internal communication and utilize the skills of a wider group of members across the different communities. Traidcraft and other external actors, such as municipal government and commercial farmers' groups, should support the development of disaster risk reduction plans and diversification of income streams.

A similarly insightful, grounded study is provided by Jason Donovan and Nigel Poole in chapter 4 which explores the specific case of the Nicaraguan coffee cooperative, Soppexcca, and associated supporting buyers and NGOs. The authors find that significant positive outcomes for the cooperative have been achieved in terms of improvements in infrastructure, membership numbers and financial stability. But there are challenges pertaining to weaknesses in cooperative governance and service provision and issues of future growth and stability. The members (especially the poorest) have not been able to intensify their coffee production and fully capitalize on the benefits of preferential market access. Both buyers and NGOs have not sufficiently questioned the impacts of their own interventions or engaged the cooperative to achieve more inclusive governance by decentralizing or delivering more effective services. More coordination and collaboration amongst stakeholders is needed, including involving buyers and NGOs in a process of mutual learning.

Said-Allsopp and Tallontire provide the third detailed case study in chapter 5, which compares a Fairtrade and a corporate code mechanism in terms of their efficacy in empowering women workers in Kenyan flowers and tea. Fairtrade has various mechanisms through which it seeks to empower workers, the most visible of which is the Joint Body. This committee decides upon the use of Fairtrade Premium funds, and is composed of representatives from management and workers. FLO (Fairtrade International) encourages equal representation of women and men amongst the workers. But many of the companies have found it difficult to achieve equal representation and women have had weak influence on decision-making in a mixed entity in the context of entrenched gender inequalities. Some of the Fairtrade Premium projects have met women's practical needs, for example funding childcare facilities, but gender bias was also exhibited in several projects which focused on issues more of interest to male than female workers, because of a lack of transparency and male dominance in decision-making.

In contrast, Gender Committees have been promoted by the Kenya Flower Council (KFC) following labour rights campaigns to give women workers greater voice in KFC code auditing. Overall, the Gender Committees have had greater success than the Joint Bodies in the cases analysed because of the support given by management, an all-women composition, broad-based training of members, encouragement to share learning with peers, and early success in tackling sexual harassment. Some have also supported rotating savings and credit associations for workers and other livelihood diversification projects, benefiting the whole community.

Surprisingly, the Joint Body, the Fairtrade tool explicitly designed to empower workers, appears so far to have been less effective than the Gender Committees which had less lofty ambitions and resulted from a more top-down process relating to social auditing in more mainstream ethical sourcing. Fairtrade is already making changes to its hired labour standard, for example requiring greater articulation with national labour legislation and social protection measures, more dialogue with trade unions to avoid undermining collective bargaining, and more flexibility in the use of the premium to reflect local conditions. But more could be done by Fairtrade to understand and respond to gender relations in the local context. Lessons can be learned from good practice in other standard systems.

Alistair Smith's chapter on access to the Fairtrade system illustrates how far the system has come in expanding the geographic scope of its operation to 70 countries. Nevertheless more needs to be done, both in extending the Fairtrade International standards to some of the least developed countries that have not yet been reached at all, and by enabling certain products that are currently only certified in a limited number of countries to be produced and certified more widely. This is particularly important because, given the growing demand for goods certified by Fairtrade International in some markets, producers unable to access certification and reach these markets consider themselves to be disadvantaged. This is the opinion of stakeholders working with NASFAM, the National Smallholder Farmers' Association of Malawi, described in a case study in this chapter.

Chapter 7 explores the current invisibility of hired labourers in certified global value chains. Smallholder farmers often rely upon temporary workers in diverse sets of institutional arrangements. Casual workers on smallholder farms may not be able to benefit from sustainability standards, because the latter tend to work with and through farmer organizations, and membership of these organizations usually means access to land title. The chapter explores cases from various sectors, including tea, sugar, non-timber forest products, coffee, cocoa, and cotton to demonstrate the varied terms of integration for hired labourers in global value chains. The authors conclude that more research is needed on the horizontal labour relations of specific geographies and on informal worker organization and agency and how sustainability standards can improve their reach.

Chapter 8 presents the views of a fair trade business owner. Adam Brett established Tropical Wholefoods in 1990 and his chapter reflects on the changes in development fashions in the last 25 years as well as the swings in commodity markets that fair trade is intended to cushion. He considers the impacts of fair trade and concludes that the most important benefits are the enduring business relationships that provide farmers with a certain degree of stability and security. Their grown-up children, often educated to a high level, are evidence of the long-term stable incomes that have been achieved.

The debate 'Does Fairtrade have more impact than conventional trade or trade certified by other sustainability standards' rounds off the collection. Matthew Anderson argues that despite some limitations, Fairtrade is a unique tool for promoting development and empowerment of marginalized rural communities in the South. Philip Booth and Sushil Mohan counter that while Fairtrade is a welcome addition to markets because it opens up alternative trade channels which meet the needs of some producers, it will never reach the very poorest farmers, it will remain a niche market, and it is not tackling market fundamentals. Other factors such as free trade, peace and stability, are far more relevant than Fairtrade when assessing relative contributions to poverty reduction in developing countries. It is conventional trade, they argue, that sets the demand and supply conditions for Fairtrade products (as well as for other VSS certified products and speciality market producers) and in which mainstream corporates and retailers have increasing power.

While accepting the positive poverty impacts of conventional trade and enterprise, Anderson points to the limited trickle down of benefits to smallholders in many global value chains and says that changing market fundamentals takes time. He suggests that the role of Fairtrade as moral entrepreneur, disrupting institutions and creating new ones, is somewhat undervalued (something Nelson and Martin also refer to in their chapter, calling it 'discursive impact', i.e. the influence of Fairtrade on the broader narratives which frame understandings of sustainability and fairness in trade). Scaling up is the overriding challenge for Fairtrade, but Anderson gives examples of retailers and major brands switching major product lines to Fairtrade certification as indications of potential future growth. However, for Booth and Sushil, while Fairtrade in itself is a positive institution, more improvements in broader policy and institutional enabling environments and reductions in trade barriers in poor economies should be the focus in development, with Fairtrade being of little relevance.

Essentially, all of the chapters in this book point to the need for Fairtrade to learn more about its effectiveness in different value chain contexts and places and to find ways to respond in a more flexible, adaptive manner to local conditions and to look more deeply at its underlying assumptions. Fairtrade has to provide assurance to buyers, which has in the past meant standardization. But unless Fairtrade can demonstrate strong impact, then the risk of not acting, of not improving producer support and of not changing and being more flexible and adaptive, could challenge Fairtrade's credibility.

Fairtrade cannot overcome deeply embedded structural and institutional constraints on its own and does not claim to. But it needs to be more strategic in its collaboration with, or advocacy of external stakeholders. Achieving this engagement with the key stakeholders in a particular locality or territory in itself requires resources, facilitation skills, and a willingness on the part of other stakeholders to engage. Fairtrade is supporting decentralization via its regional producer networks and in some cases through newly emerging national networks, but this type of brokering (or support for ongoing stakeholder participatory processes) needs to happen at the local or sub-regional level as well, anchored in a full understanding of the local context and its dynamics and characteristics. A reconnection with political economy more fundamentally is also overdue – Fairtrade's move into the mainstream does not enable it to tackle agribusiness concentration in global value chains. Tackling poverty has to mean tackling the root causes of farmers' and workers' vulnerability.

A capacity and willingness to rethink strategies and approaches may ultimately be required within Fairtrade, if impact and case studies continue to point to challenges within its current mode of operation. Increasingly, Fairtrade will be compared against its peers – other voluntary standard systems, and indeed other market-based mechanisms and alternative approaches in addition to Fairtrade (i.e. combined with) or that do not involve certification at all.

Fairtrade does already constantly revise its standards and approaches, and it is important to recognize that in a participatory stakeholder movement, consultation and consensus take time. Capturing the benefits of the wider Fairtrade International organization – beyond specific impact studies in particular places – also requires more attention. But the question is, can Fairtrade learn deeply and fast enough? Can it recognize where there are limitations in its current approach and make the right changes? If not, then it may struggle to retain its relevance and credibility. The mainstreaming process has led Fairtrade International along a certain path, which arguably now opens it to risks of being sidelined by the new strategies of international companies which may focus upon own-brand initiatives. In the end the important thing is not the survival of Fairtrade International *per se*, although the institutional development of the Fairtrade system is now highly advanced. The priority should be either the continuation of a more agile, relational Fairtrade system or the creation of a more powerful international social movement that can challenge the structures and institutions of unfair trade and quickly.

About the author

Valerie Nelson is Principal Researcher at the Natural Resources Institute, University of Greenwich, UK.

CHAPTER 2

Exploring issues of rigour and utility in Fairtrade impact assessment

Valerie Nelson and Adrienne Martin

Abstract

This chapter explores the evolution of Fairtrade impact assessment, which reflects the wider context of international development evaluation practice and debates. Appropriate designs and methods in evaluation are hotly contested, ultimately reflecting different development philosophies and values. Earlier Fairtrade impact studies were primarily case studies involving qualitative methods. As Fairtrade has grown and scrutiny from different stakeholders has increased, there has been increased demand for more rigour and criticism of studies that do not include a 'credible' counterfactual. More recently, there have been increasing numbers of impact evaluation studies using mixed designs as well as mixed methods. But challenges remain as to how to balance utility and rigour in Fairtrade impact assessment, because there are trade-offs in terms of skill and resource requirements and in relation to ethical issues. Yet all sustainability standards are being asked to both demonstrate impact and to inform impact. Achieving utility not only at higher levels of organizations in Fairtrade, but also for producers at the local level is a significant challenge, when 'credibility' in impact assessment is judged in some quarters as being the same as using counterfactual logics. In many cases the construction of a counterfactual is very difficult if not impossible. In this paper we seek to provide some practical suggestions for improving both rigour and utility.

Keywords: Fairtrade, impact assessment, sustainability standards, evaluation, fair trade

FAIRTRADE HAS GROWN RAPIDLY in recent decades and this has led to increased scrutiny of its impact by researchers, donors, and the press. This paper explores how Fairtrade impact assessment has evolved. Firstly we provide a brief overview of the evolution of monitoring and evaluation in international development more generally and then we chart the development of impact evaluation and learning in Fairtrade. We identify some of the specific challenges posed for impact assessment for this particular standard system and discuss the ways in which scholars and practitioners are seeking to improve rigour and/or utility – both of which have been lacking in the past to varying degrees in many studies. There are difficulties in achieving both improved rigour and utility

http://dx.doi.org/10.3362/9781780449067.002

simultaneously, because there are often trade-offs involved. However, we seek to show some practical ways of doing this. This chapter draws on secondary literature and on the authors' own extensive experience of impact assessment generally and specifically in Fairtrade, and sustainability standards.

The evolution of impact evaluation in the wider international development context

Fairtrade impact assessment reflects overall practice in evaluation in international development. Between the 1950s and 1970s there was little study of development impact and effectiveness: 'the (assumed) need for aid was seen as a sufficient basis for providing it' (Riddell, 2009 cited in Ramalingam, 2011: 1). Early impact assessments were *ex ante* economic, social, environmental impact assessments conducted *before* a project to scope the potential impacts of an intervention to inform funding decisions. *Ex post* impact assessments emerged in time, with a time lag of several years after project end (Roche, 1999). During the 1970s and 1980s project planning tools emerged, such as logical frameworks. Logical frameworks present the main elements of a project, the links between them, and notes risks and assumptions, with widespread uptake in the 1990s, driven by donors, focusing on results and delivery. This approach possibly focused attention on project deliverables, potentially diverting attention from social change processes (Edward and Tallontire, 2009).

During the 1980s and 1990s participatory approaches emerged in development, including in impact assessment (for example see Guijt et al., 1998; Estrella et al., 2000). Interpretations of participation have varied from approaches which support appreciative enquiry and a learning process guided by participants' own interests and decisions to approaches which rely only on consultation of beneficiaries and which tend to conflate a participatory *process* with specific participatory rural appraisal (PRA) techniques. While there was a flowering of participatory approaches and ideas, many multilateral agencies stopped short of adopting 'extended' participation and instead allowed only 'limited participation' in impact assessment (Roche, 1999: 19). The values of participatory development infer that a 'pluralist, evolutionary and iterative' approach to evaluation is important. They can be rigorous and include both qualitative and quantitative techniques and, crucially, they give greater voice to those affected by a project and much more weight to their experiences when compared with conventional methods (Chambers, 2009). The ideas and values of participatory development have had a major impact on international development, including in evaluation. However, the gains achieved in the 1990s and 2000s by proponents are also under pressure from the new focus on evidence, certain interpretations of rigour, and impact evaluation which we explain below.

During the 1990s impact assessment became more systematic, with a greater focus on outcomes and consequences of a project. There were increased efforts to define and measure impact and lots of activities and debate, but still a lack of progress in understanding impacts and no overarching evidence to provide a clear steer to policy-makers on what works (Riddell, 2007; Ramalingam, 2011). Donor projects were, for the first time, assessed against their logframe outputs and outcomes. The increased pressure on NGOs to demonstrate results and impact led to exaggerations of achievements by some and overblown criticisms by opponents (Roche, 1999). A lack of professional norms and standards in the sector, a growing demand for high profile and press coverage to raise funds, and poor institutional learning systems and weak accountability mechanisms led to a widening gap between agency rhetoric and the realities of what had been achieved. This in turn contributed to growing scepticism of the value of aid and exposed NGOs to public criticism and the odd polemical attack (Roche, 1999). Demand for greater accountability and learning in donor-led interventions was also growing in this period, with some innovations such as outcome-oriented approaches. Outcome Mapping, developed by the International Development Research Centre (Earl et al., 2001), for example, tracks changes in knowledge, attitudes, and practices, rather than more traditional impact indicators such as income and productivity in recognition of complexity and to promote learning.

In the 1990s the scientific realism school of evaluation developed. Pawson and Tilley (1997) of the scientific realist school argued that experimental and quasi-experimental methods never reach expectations and they critique 'the epistemological assumptions about causation and their lack of fit with the nature of social programs' (Pawson and Tilley, 1997: 30). Ramalingam (2011: 1) concurs that initially ambitious studies have often had to be 'scaled back, narrowed in scope and made "more realistic", in the face of the complex realities of development efforts. As a result, the arguments for and against the effectiveness of aid policies and practices remained patchy, partial and inconclusive'. By focusing on the mechanisms by which an intervention seeks to effect change (articulated in a theory of change) a more realistic understanding of impact can be achieved (Pawson and Tilley, 1997). Recently, Eyben (2013) has cautioned against the use of theories of change in a mechanistic way and merely replicating linear logical framework assumptions of how change happens. With theories of change and theory-based evaluation currently in vogue, it is important to remember that these are just tools and they need to be used in a process of learning which leads to rethinking assumptions and making changes to strategies, where evaluations show existing assumptions do not hold and current strategies are not working.

In the 2000s there has been a significant rise of 'an evidence agenda' among donors and development agencies (Garbarino and Holland, 2009) with growing demands for 'rigorous' evidence on the impact of development interventions to inform policy-makers and to justify aid budgets. In the next section we further explore this focus on rigour in monitoring and evaluation among aid agencies and some evaluation specialists.

The new focus on rigour in impact studies

Increased attention is being paid to improving rigour in impact assessment and to understanding 'what works' to increase aid impact. While few would argue with the overall goal, there are issues in terms of how this is achieved. There are also important divergences in how rigour is understood.

Among many researchers, evaluators, and aid agencies rigour is most associated with experimental and quasi-experimental approaches involving statistical surveys of controlled comparisons between treatment and control groups. Value for money assessments in planning stages and formal impact evaluation are increasingly required by some donors. Such approaches restrict impact assessment to assessing the magnitude of change which is specifically attributable to a programme or intervention, rather than broader approaches which define impact as learning about change processes, involving before and after comparisons, but not necessarily employing counterfactuals, i.e. what might have happened without an intervention.

3iE is an organization supported by several donors and its own rapid growth trajectory and (evolving) interpretation of rigour reflects the way in which rigour has come to the fore in international development evaluation. For example, 3iE sees only studies with credible counterfactuals and with a design based on the underlying programme theory to learn what works, why, and at what cost as being up to standard (3iE website). This does not only mean experimental and quasi-experimental designs, but these are now central to what is considered high quality evidence by donors, 3iE, and many evaluation specialists.

But some researchers and practitioners have highlighted that randomized control trials (RCTs) and quasi-experimental designs are not appropriate for some types of interventions, are costly, and have flaws. For example, while they might give strong evidence of whether an intervention had an impact in a particular place, they are weak on issues of replication elsewhere. In this more sophisticated understanding of rigour, rigour is not determined solely by the use of a particular method, but rather the appropriateness of the 'fit' between the nature of the problem being assessed and the particular methods (singular or in combination) used in response to the problem, and the time, political, financial, ethical, and logistical constraints (Patton, 2008; Woolcock et al., 2010). Interventions vary in their characteristics, with more complex interventions necessitating different evaluation designs compared with more simple examples (e.g. vaccination programmes).

While some argue that credible evidence can *only* be generated by experimental and quasi-experimental designs (see for example Blackman and Rivera, 2010), others proffer a broader set of designs which may be appropriate for different situations and may have *equivalent* robustness and credibility. In their DFID review, Stern et al. (2012) provide an overview of different evaluation designs and the logics upon which they rely, as well as the mix of methods which can be employed. Thus, while many would assume that a counterfactual is the basis of any evaluation (the rules of causal inference to support causal claims stemming from a comparison between carefully selected treatment and control groups), there are other understandings of causation that can be used. Theory-based evaluation draws on generative causation as its rules for causal inference. In a holistic way it interrogates the mechanism being employed: 'How does it work? Which elements are important?' and 'How can it be improved? (Befani, 2012; Yin, 2014). It is of course possible to mix not just methods but designs so that the strengths of one can complement the flaws of the other and vice versa.

In terms of mixing methods there has also been recent and growing convergence between qualitative and quantitative approaches to data generation. Examples include the quantification of stakeholder perceptions, the use of software to code qualitative data to make it more manageable for analysis, and participatory generation of numbers. Holland (2013), for example, provides multiple examples of participatory statistics that aggregate data gathered from individuals using PRA tools in group settings. The traditional distinction could therefore be recast as 'data collected from structured, closed-ended questions and non-structured, open-ended, modes of enquiry' (Woolcock et al., 2010: 3). While many evaluations in the past have focused on the specific inputs and outputs of a project or programme, theory-based evaluation considers the whole chain. There are also methods for analysing the other plausible interventions or contextual factors which have created change, as well as the initiative being evaluated, such as contribution analysis. However, less structured techniques are emerging which instead essentially ask, 'What changes have happened here?', and only secondarily ask, 'what factors caused these changes?' They thus seek to assess the impact of an initiative in a more participatory, less structured way and may therefore deliver a less biased assessment. At the same time the direct and detailed causal mechanisms may become less clear to evaluators and perhaps less easy to improve.

The expectation of many donors of rigour in studies which they commission, involving 'credible' counterfactuals, theory-based evaluation or mixed designs, and of mixed methods has substantial resource and skill implications. These approaches are costly and require sophisticated skills both in advanced statistics and quantitative techniques, but also in qualitative methods and in combining all of these together to answer evaluation questions. The level of investment may not always be appropriate in the context of non-governmental organizations – certainly for smaller ones. For first generation studies aimed at informing policy there may be more justification (Stern et al., 2012), but this approach is both hard to resource and hard to justify for smaller organizations.

Balancing accountability with participation is also a critical issue here and adds to the challenges for those commissioning and undertaking studies. The methods involved in rigorous studies of the kind proposed by 3iE and many donors tend toward the more extractive end of the spectrum and can distance interviewees from the research process itself. Ethical issues arise in experimental methods (who gets treatment and who does not is a particularly loaded issue where participants are already disadvantaged). Quasi-experimental methods are also less likely to support ongoing learning, participation, and flexibility. These techniques take up the time of participants, without them being involved in decision-making or seeing any immediate benefits, and resources may be diverted away from support for participants' own processes of learning. Balancing accountability and learning objectives for participants is thus tricky. Proponents of rigorous experimental and quasi-experimental approaches would argue that in the longer-term much larger numbers of people will benefit from policies which are more informed by evidence. Some policy questions merit such an intensive approach, but only for 'first generation' studies – i.e. once a base level of evidence has been gathered it should not be necessary to keep repeating the studies (Stern et al., 2012). Much therefore depends upon the overall priorities for the study.

However, the generation of evidence is only one part of policy-making, which is itself a messy, non-linear process. The existence of rigorous evidence does not guarantee that it shapes final decisions on policy processes – which should be publicly debated and driven by values, but which are also influenced by many other factors and interest groups. The framing of which type of policy option on which to gather evidence is also an important issue: there are dominant policy narratives at work and these frame the nature of the evidence collected. We see this reflected perhaps in the much greater scrutiny of Fairtrade compared with other sustainability standards and market mechanisms to date, for example, because of its high visibility and marketing as an alternative form of trade. A critical current is emerging from some NGOs, practitioners and academics who are challenging a results and evidence agenda which they think neglects the power dimensions involved and which presents evidence generation and use as a neutral, technical exercise alone. In fact, evidence can be misrepresented, is often inconclusive, and can be used in a partial manner to suit interests. According to Eyben (2013) official aid agencies tend to focus on measuring effectiveness in a way that assumes problems are bounded and simple, with their emphasis on linear cause–effect logical planning. Power relations, complexity, surprises, and unexpected impacts and the partiality of knowledge are neglected (Eyben, 2013). However, while this may be true in the past, it is our experience that there are also changes occurring within donors and in the development debate. For example, there is recognition within DFID of a wide set of evaluation approaches (see Stern et al., 2012). In our experience this is also influencing their terms of reference for evaluations of market-based interventions, which take account of challenges to complexity and the need for mixed designs and methods.

Complexity and its implications are currently in the spotlight in development debates with implications for evaluation, as well as aid in general (see for example Ramalingam, 2013). Complex systems are a collection of parts, but collectively they have a range of dimensions; the parts share a physical or symbolic environment or space, and action by any part can affect the whole

(Ramalingam, 2008). This means that spillover effects are highly likely and creating a counterfactual as the sole basis for evaluation design and measurement becomes problematic, because the comparison between treatment and control group can be invalidated. It is rarely possible (or desirable) to exert control over treatment and control groups in private sector-led interventions and longitudinal studies are particularly challenging. Thus, different approaches may be needed, such as theory-based evaluation, but also changes in the way monitoring and evaluation is commissioned and positioned vis-à-vis the entity being evaluated.

The development of Fairtrade impact assessment

This broader backdrop of monitoring and evaluation, the evidence agenda, and tensions between accountability and learning approaches and objectives provides the context for sustainability standards, such as Fairtrade, as they have firstly recognized and secondly sought to assess their impact. The evolution of Fairtrade impact assessment reflects the wider picture in international development, although Fairtrade, as a market-based mechanism, has perhaps lagged behind practice in international NGOs. In this section we explore how Fairtrade impact assessment has evolved and identify some of the specific challenges posed.

Early studies of fair trade in the late 1990s were fairly exploratory and covered cases which could be termed fair or ethical trade (see NRET, 1999; Roberts et al., 1999). A number of in-depth, qualitative studies on fair trade followed in the early 2000s: for example Ronchi (2002a) conducted an impact study in Costa Rica and a participatory monitoring and evaluation (M&E) exercise with a certified Ghanaian cocoa cooperative funded by the alternative trade organization called Twin (Ronchi, 2002b). The first comparative studies – those that compared outcomes and impacts of conventional and fair or ethical trading chains in Peruvian brazil nuts and Ecuadorian cocoa (Nelson et al., 2002) – did not involve counterfactuals in a statistical sense, but provided comparisons that were qualitative in nature and helped to tackle some research bias issues, and identified stakeholder groups being neglected by the fair trade scheme being studied.

During the mid- to late 2000s, a series of rich case studies was undertaken (see the meta reviews of Nelson and Pound, 2009 and the ITC, 2011 review of sustainability standards impact on producers) including some very in-depth studies (see for example, Jaffee, 2007), but few involved the kinds of counterfactual logics described above. Ruben et al. (2008) is one key exception. By 2009 there had been a proliferation of studies. Nelson and Pound (2009) found a number of gaps in the evidence base including a dearth of Asian and African studies, few non-coffee studies, the lack of attention to gender and environmental impacts, and noted the mainly qualitative nature of the studies undertaken. To our knowledge there were no theory-based evaluations.

In 2010 Blackman and Rivera reviewed the evidence on sustainability standards in agricultural commodities and tourism to establish whether these standards improve the social and environmental performance of farms and firms. They identified *ex post* empirical farm level studies and classified them according to whether they employed methods likely to generate credible results. Their definition of credible studies was based on the inclusion of a counterfactual; that is, studies with an experimental or quasi-experimental design (e.g. the latter involving matching of certified producers and non-certified producers and using advanced statistical techniques to address potential selection bias, such as propensity score matching; see Ruben et al., 2008). The latter approach requires large numbers of observations and therefore can be expensive, and as a result it means the coverage of a wide-ranging system such as Fairtrade is very limited, with findings drawn from a small number of organizations. It is also the case that quasi-experimental studies which are not nested within a mixed methods and theory-based approach cannot explain very well how and why outcomes and impacts have been achieved. Many detailed case studies are dismissed as irrelevant when they do not involve counterfactuals in this way, but this seems to ignore both the light they can shed on causal mechanisms and, when used systematically in comparative analysis, the fact that they can allow researchers to generalize (although not to universalize) beyond one particular situation.

Case studies may be the only option in some situations where the construction of a counterfactual is just not possible. In one study (B. Pound, unpublished internal report) for the Fairtrade Foundation, the researchers found that all of the farmers in a particular industry fell within a certain producer organization which holds Fairtrade certification (Belize sugar). Therefore, there is no counterfactual at all.

It is increasingly the case that in some industries and countries all producer organizations are now certified to one sustainability standard or another. If they are not yet certified it is because they sell on a different market or are newly established; that is, they exhibit characteristics which mean they are not a valid comparison. In some way they are not a good match for the organizations which are certified. This situation is only likely to increase as certification expands in different sectors. In this context it is necessary to move to the next best level of counterfactual – namely the non-certified farmers in similar zones and of similar characteristics who do not sell through an organization, but who sell directly to intermediary traders. It is possible that organizations change their certification status during the study and this means the comparisons are undermined, with some taking up new certifications, others stacking up multiple certifications, and others dropping them when they are deemed no longer useful. The comparisons between the certified and non-certified producers may still have some value, but only where a detailed qualitative analysis using theory-based evaluation is also conducted to explain how and why changes are occurring. This has resource implications. While it may be desirable to have high levels of rigour, it is not always practical or achievable given the nature of and patterns of distribution of certified groups in Fairtrade.

The development of theories of change by researchers and standard systems is now helping to provide some structure to studies operating in such high levels of complexity. It is significant that Fairtrade International has now developed its own theory of change and indicators, which will improve its own monitoring of results, can provide greater clarity for researchers, and will enable more standardization across cases to build up a stronger picture overall – even where studies are conducted by different researchers or standard representatives. Complexity in the Fairtrade system stems from the broad reaching nature of the standards, as well as the variation in the other inputs which vary over time and are less standardized (e.g. producer support, networking, and growing markets). In other words Fairtrade has multiple impact pathways. The inputs are also fairly volatile in market-based interventions – the Fairtrade Minimum Price is only active when market prices fall below it and at other times may provide price uplifts for individual farmers, but benefits to individuals also depend upon the operating costs and relative efficiency of the producer organization in returning benefits to members. The Fairtrade Premium is generated according to what a producer organization can sell – and this will vary according to market demand for Fairtrade-certified products and the willingness of buyers to buy from the specific producer organization. The particular training provided by the producer support services of Fairtrade may also vary from place to place. Critically, the additional support provided by external NGOs, alternative trade organizations, and donors varies from place to place. The impact trajectory of Fairtrade will also vary over time – there may be significant early gains prior to certification in the preparation phase, for example, and while continuous improvement is intended, there may be significant jumps or setbacks for different contextual reasons. The uptake of Fairtrade co-produces outcomes in interaction with the local context (Neilson and Pritchard, 2009; see also Nelson and Martin, 2012 on the factors shaping the impact of Fairtrade). For example, individual farmers' views of their producer organization can be shaped by the history of cooperatives in that particular country, as well as their current performance.

Studies which try to manage all of this complexity are highly challenging for researchers, but also for those commissioning the studies (donors and Fairtrade organizations), because the findings may not be as clear as they would like. Many rigorous studies are unable to establish statistically significant differences between those certified with sustainability standards and those not certified at individual household level. Many impact evaluations in this field are showing mixed results, although this does not mean that no impacts are being achieved. Further, there is a risk of generalizing from too few cases across a whole standard system. Given the breadth of the Fairtrade system, which currently spans 70 countries, building up evidence will take time and should not consume disproportionate amounts of resources in comparison with those invested by consumers, companies, donors, and others in the Fairtrade system. A recent impact evaluation of Fairtrade and Rainforest Alliance is both multi-year and multi-enterprise, but the findings are still restricted to two commodities and four countries (see Nelson and Martin, 2013a). The cost and challenges of employing mixed designs should not be under-estimated. Policy-makers and Fairtrade organizations frequently want clearer, less nuanced findings than can be realistically delivered by such studies – especially when given an ambitious scope at the outset.

Participatory statistics provide one way in which participatory approaches and impact evaluation can converge (see Holland, 2013). Community level data can be generated to assess livelihood outcomes, as well as process issues, and this data can be more accurate than small numbers of responses from community leaders or individual households. Thus accuracy is a key aspect of this debate. However, it is also the case that participatory statistics and qualitative data need to be representative, otherwise inaccuracies can occur and received wisdom about what works may go unchallenged. For example, a reliance on village case studies rather than nationally representative surveys led many social scientists to inaccurately interpret the impacts of the Green Revolution in Bangladesh, according to Orr (2013).

Improving rigour in Fairtrade impact assessment

The choice of design for an impact study should be about aligning evaluation questions with the tools and methods which are available and the specific features or attributes of the intervention being studied (Stern et al., 2012). Misalignment between methods, questions, and attributes can mean that the evaluation cannot actually answer the questions posed by the study. The ethos or development philosophy of the organization commissioning or undertaking the study is also relevant. Many organizations, including Fairtrade ones, face difficult choices about which objectives (learning or accountability) to prioritize, as these two objectives do not always sit easily together and resources are limited. Some NGOs have taken a public stance to focus only on learning-based evaluation as a matter of principle. Solidaridad, a Dutch international NGO, has opted for 'improving not proving' (Solidaridad Network, Annual Report, 2012), although this does not render them immune from external criticism of a lack of rigour and therefore credibility in their evaluation findings.

When selecting an approach to impact assessment, the focus has been on mixing methods, but mixing of designs is also possible. All evaluations draw upon an idea of what causes change (they have a specific understanding of causality, even if this is not explicitly articulated). Statistical surveys rely on controlled comparisons and quasi-experimental and experimental methods with carefully selected treatment and control groups. In this type of study the counterfactual is the 'without treatment' group. However, it is not always easy to sustain these groups when private sector companies are involved as they may decide to drop or take up new certifications or decide not to continue participating in the study. Spillover effects are also common, with practices taken

up by one group copied by others in the same industry. These resource-inten-
sive studies can help us to understand the extent of impact in a particular
location, but are weak at explaining whether the approach might work elsewhere. Experimental and quasi-experimental designs require large numbers of
observations. This is not often the situation when studying Fairtrade, or other
sustainability standards. At the organizational level there are limited numbers of certified and non-certified organizations that could be matched and
Fairtrade works through the producer organization. At the individual member
level higher numbers may be found but only in some instances and a focus
only on the individual members fails to capture the role of the producer organization in shaping impact and the diversity among producer organizations.

Theory-based evaluation is an alternative in such situations and such
approaches are based on generative causation; that is, the 'mechanisms'
employed as a whole in a case are identified and detailed analysis is carried out
to understand how these have generated effects and how much other explana-
tions are responsible (Nelson and Martin, 2011). In a recent study conducted
for Fairtrade we explored the impact of Fairtrade on cocoa in Peru (Laroche
et al., forthcoming). In such an approach the focus is on generating data along
the theory of change, focusing on the transitions (e.g. have the inputs led to
outputs and so on) to build a rigorous 'within case' analysis. The influence
of context grows as one moves along the theory of change, which means
that it is usually more feasible to provide rigorous attribution only on the
earlier phases of the theory of change (i.e. inputs and outputs) and to provide
validation of plausible outcomes and impacts at the latter stages – where both
broader contextual factors and alternative interventions contribute. Theory-
based evaluation is strong on explanation, but weaker on estimating quantities or the extent of impact (Stern et al., 2012).

It is possible to combine designs which are complementary to strengthen
the overall study (Stern et al., 2012; Yin, 2014). For example, in a DFID-funded
study of the poverty impact of sustainability standards (Nelson and Martin,
2013a) we covered multiple cases at country-industry level and compared
these in a systematic way. We included multiple producer organizations in
each country and compared them systematically also. In each country we
included non-participating producer organizations and companies and collected data at both certified and non-certified entities to allow for comparisons (quasi-experimental study). This represents a nested and mixed design,
with diverse methods also used, and so the findings are as rigorous as they
can be in light of the complexity inherent within sustainability standards
and in the different contexts of study. One approach which may be promising for Fairtrade and which has not yet been tried is qualitative comparative
analysis (QCA). QCA is useful for identifying which causes and conditions
are necessary and sufficient to achieve certain outcomes. This type of analysis could be used with sets of case studies, where the number of case studies
makes it difficult for a researcher to manage them comfortably, and as a way
of teasing out the aspects of an intervention and the contextual conditions

for success (Ragin, 1987) – something which has eluded many Fairtrade case study researchers to date.

There are a number of practical steps to improving rigour which could be considered. Firstly, the development of a research protocol is important. If more than one case is being covered in the impact study it is important to employ standardized questions to support cross-comparative analysis. The theory of change already provides a level of standardization, but it is important to ensure that the evaluation questions and research propositions are clearly articulated (Yin, 2014). A research protocol can then be developed to guide each country team. While this sounds prescriptive it need not be so if there is sufficient time and effort undertaken to engage all those involved in conducting the study in the design, although it is unlikely to support a participatory learning process driven by farmers and workers. A protocol can support shared understanding within the research team, clarity on how Fairtrade works, and communication of the study objectives. As well as the theory of change and priority evaluation questions, it should specify the relevant indicators to be used (including scope for participatory indicator development), the data collection strategies and process, the analytical strategies, the writing up process (responsibilities and structure of report), and feedback processes and opportunities.

Secondly, stakeholders, especially producers and workers, can be engaged in analysing whether the intended theory of change of Fairtrade has indeed led to intended outcomes and impacts. However, this can be time consuming and fairly challenging and requires careful explanation and adequate time allocation. An alternative is to ask in a more open way what has generated change, with the contribution of Fairtrade explored secondarily. As Fairtrade works along the value chain it is important that impact studies engage with and consider the full value chain in understanding whether intended inputs and outputs have led to outcomes and impacts. While this has been relatively neglected or under-resourced in many studies, greater attention is being paid with methodologies being developed to quantify perceptions of change in terms of the 'fairness' of the value chain relationships (see Unilever et al., 2012; Twin, 2012) and given many of the difficulties in obtaining commercially sensitive information from value chain actors. The use of theory of change and diverse stakeholder participation in assessing change and its different causes using new techniques such as contribution analysis (Mayne, 2008) is a potentially powerful approach and one that may increase rigour. Because the Fairtrade theory of change is complex it is important to ensure that impact studies focus on priority evaluation questions, particular impact pathways or specific themes, otherwise the study is likely to become too ambitious and may find it difficult to answer the questions adequately.

Thirdly, new methods are emerging which could be applied in the Fairtrade field. Process tracing methods, for example, are 'tools to study causal mechanisms in a single case research design' (Beach and Pedersen, 2013: 2; Oxfam, 2013). Once a rigorous 'within case' analysis is built up for different cases these can be systematically compared. Typologies can be used to guide the selection of cases and support wider conclusions to be drawn than unconnected case studies, although not universal answers (Yin, 2014; George and Bennett, 2005). For sustainability standards such as Fairtrade, it is possible to develop a typology as we are currently doing in a coffee impact study for Fairtrade International of the types of producer organizations in Fairtrade coffee and selecting from these. QCA has not been used as yet in Fairtrade or sustainability standard impact studies, but offers the potential to review a larger number of cases and to establish the necessary and sufficient conditions for the achievement of specific outcomes (Ragin, 1987). This may be a useful approach because Fairtrade is such a wide-ranging system, exhibiting inherent complexities, and it is important that advances are made in understanding not whether it works or not, but in a more nuanced way we need to know how well it works under different conditions and how it can be improved.

Assessing the relative contribution of plausible rival interventions or contextual factors should be part of the discussion and analysis at each point in the theory of change to establish their relative significance in bringing about impact (Stern et al., 2012). We have done this in an impact evaluation with key informants, but it could be done more explicitly with multiple stakeholders in a workshop (Nelson and Martin, 2013a). Contribution analysis (Mayne, 2008) is a participatory technique which can be used to assess the relative contribution of different interventions to change processes. In relation to Fairtrade, this technique is particularly important because other NGO, donor, and private sector initiatives commonly invest in producer organizations as well as, and often because of, Fairtrade. While many impact studies have noted this (e.g. Nelson and Smith, 2010a), it is also the case that few have attempted to engage stakeholders in quantifying their perceptions of relative contribution and more could be done in this regard.

Local stakeholder workshops are useful, not just for feedback, but as part of the process of data gathering, to draw in diverse stakeholder perspectives including farmers and workers. In an ongoing Fairtrade coffee study, we have used force field analysis to understand how producer organization board managers and leaders see their organizations changing over recent years and the negative and positive forces shaping this trajectory of change.

At an organizational level, where producer groups have already developed clear plans and strategies of their own and collect key data for monitoring, it is easier to build upon this with the impact study. Outcome mapping could also contribute to producer organization learning and contribute to mixed method evaluations. While it is important not to conflate participatory rural appraisal (PRA) methods with a participatory *process,* it is the case that some methods are more understandable to many rural farmers where there are high levels of illiteracy. For example, participatory gross margin analysis, also being trialled in an ongoing Fairtrade coffee impact study, is a technique for estimating the costs and benefits of a specific enterprise with a group of carefully selected farmers, in a way that is of value to them.

Development of poverty ladders and rural typologies is an area where more innovation is also urgently needed. This is because while Fairtrade often brings positive benefits, impact evaluations are indicating that poverty impacts – moving significant numbers of disadvantaged groups up the poverty ladder – are less likely (Nelson and Martin, 2013a). Therefore, a focus on the wider picture and the structural challenges for Fairtrade, producer organizations, and wider stakeholders in a locality is important. Overlapping and complementary interventions will be needed to tackle poverty far beyond Fairtrade (Vorley et al., 2013). An analysis of rural differentiation is important and impact studies can be enriched by seeking to understand this bigger picture.

While specific Fairtrade impact studies may need to focus on specific themes or priority questions, it is important that the different scales at which Fairtrade operates are taken into account in the wider debate on its effectiveness. Too often Fairtrade has been valued based on its impact for certified producers and workers alone. Yet there are different scales at which Fairtrade operates (see Figure 2.1). As well as the impacts at individual and organizational level, there

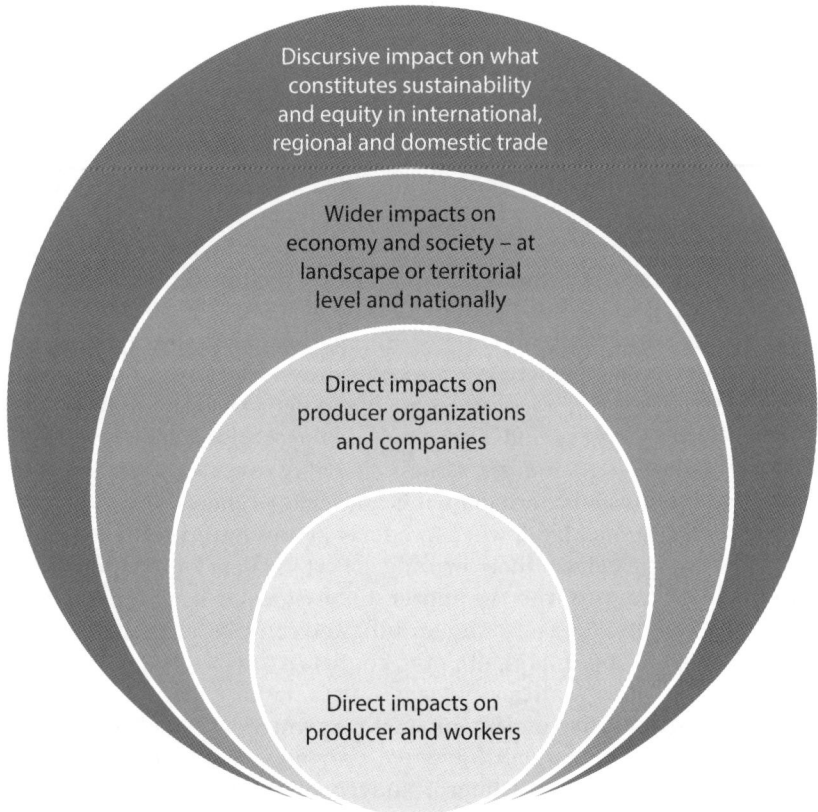

Discursive impact on what constitutes sustainability and equity in international, regional and domestic trade

Wider impacts on economy and society – at landscape or territorial level and nationally

Direct impacts on producer organizations and companies

Direct impacts on producer and workers

Figure 2.1 Different types or scales of Fairtrade impact

may be wider impacts in the local economy. Spillover effects can occur in the local community or beyond (e.g. others may benefit from the improvement of a school or crop collection centres). Demonstration and learning effects are also common: For example, new agricultural practices introduced by Fairtrade and sustainability standards can spread among neighbouring farmers. Cases have been found where Fairtrade has raised prices offered by non-certified buyers of cocoa in order to compete with the certified buyers (Nelson and Galvez, 2002; Laroche et al., 2014). Thus Fairtrade can be having an impact, but a simple comparison between certified and non-certified groups would not show significant statistical differences as a result. This is why theory of change analysis and mixed methods are needed – to contextualize and explain such processes and effects (positive or negative).

Increased attention is being paid to landscape level issues in relation to sourcing decisions by companies and in monitoring and evaluation. Agri-businesses are being urged to consider 'reducing risks by adopting landscape approaches to sustainable sourcing' (Kissinger et al., 2013). This is because to protect and enhance ecosystem services requires consideration of scale effects (Tallontire et al., 2012). Assessing change at an individual farm level does not necessarily capture the cumulative effects at a wider scale: reduced pesticide use may be environmentally beneficial at the individual farm level and produce health benefits for farmers less exposed to harmful agrochemicals, but a greater carbon footprint may be the overall result; as many farmers reduce their pesticide use this can lead to more land being used and more yields lost to pests (Tallontire et al., 2012). To fully understand environmental impacts would thus require full life-cycle analysis.

There is an aspect of Fairtrade impact which tends not to be given much attention in impact studies, namely its discursive impact. In other words, Fairtrade has an influence on (and is influenced by) the discourse around agricultural trade and sustainability. As the pioneer, Fairtrade deserves credit for the later development of other sustainability standards and initiatives in agricultural food chains. Whatever the current challenges or future preferred strategies, Fairtrade and other sustainability standards have made an important contribution to putting sustainability on the agenda by building consumer, corporate, and development agency understanding and interest in sustainability issues in agri-food chains (SustainAbility, 2011). However, it is also worth noting that some sustainability issues are not currently covered by Fairtrade as part of its core approach, such as greenhouse gas emissions.

Improving utility in Fairtrade impact assessment

So far the discussion has focused on ways of improving rigour in Fairtrade impact assessment, but for moral reasons an equally important issue is that of learning and utility and for whom? The increased focus on rigour can leave utility at best neglected and at worst undermined – particularly for farmers and workers, as well as for higher level stakeholders. Different impact studies have differing objectives and therefore not all need the same levels of rigour. As a first step it is important for those considering investing in impact work to understand what is appropriate for them, given their resources and considering who will benefit and who will bear the cost of the evaluation.

It is absolutely essential to engage stakeholders in impact assessment and not to sacrifice this objective in the pursuit of rigour. But how can this be achieved given the trade-offs involved? Firstly, it is important to focus on the overall evaluation process rather than the specific methods being employed.

For Fairtrade as a wide-ranging stakeholder movement there is the opportunity to engage with stakeholders in terms of developing their overall monitoring and evaluation framework. Fairtrade International has conducted various workshops with regional producer networks, for example, in developing the theory of change and in planning indicators. Fairtrade has the most participatory governance structure of any of the voluntary sustainability standards, but it is not clear how far Southern stakeholders have been engaged in decision-making on impact assessment and the commissioning process for studies (which is when many decisions are made about the type of study which can be undertaken). As a global sustainability standard and as a member of ISEAL, Fairtrade International is developing global indicators to allow for comparative analysis linked to their theory of change, but there would also be opportunities in specific impact case studies to allow for more participatory indicator development to be undertaken. Where stakeholder engagement can be facilitated prior to commissioning this is to be encouraged. Capacity strengthening among Southern evaluation specialists in this field is also needed to support ongoing learning processes and investment is needed in producer organizations' own capacity to monitor and learn about their performance and impact.

Once a study is under way, stakeholders can be invited to directly debate the theory of change or, in a more open, less structured way, they can be asked to identify change and its causes. A compromise is to ask about organizational change over the past x years and the forces which have shaped change (positive and negative during that period).

Participation can be increased even in quasi-experimental studies which are mixed with qualitative methods by engaging key stakeholders, including producers and workers, in the research process. This is particularly important in situations of complexity, as is the case with Fairtrade impact assessments which have to take account of multiple impact pathways, diverse partnerships, plausible alternative interventions, and highly variable contextual conditions. By holding a stakeholder meeting, key informant interviews, and using PRA techniques this can support engagement by farmers, workers, and broader stakeholders. The purpose of the study can be fully explained, time given to gathering diverse stakeholder perspectives, and a feedback process established. There is less scope though for supporting learning by farmers and workers as it is not a process driven by their own learning and there are constraints on what can be changed and adapted in terms of the evaluation design if rigour is to be sustained.

Within the Fairtrade system there are possibilities for participatory methods to be used, such as value chain dialogues or participatory video, to support producer and worker communication along the value chain and with Fairtrade International, even within a mixed design or method evaluation, but only if resources are available. The more attention given to farmers' and workers' voices the better. While some studies adopt a more participatory approach, the voices of farmers and workers are still filtered through researchers and presented in reports. There is scope to use and adapt participatory video approaches to overcome literacy barriers at the local level and to cross distances in terms of communicating issues. How far such approaches can effect change depends upon the willingness of Fairtrade actors to act upon the findings.

For a longer-term strategy and where Fairtrade itself is funding impact studies there is scope to build up relationships in a particular sub-region, landscape, or territory. Fairtrade could support a learning alliance to emerge, involving stakeholders at this more localized level in which a producer organization or estate is located, to support a process of learning linked to action. Such a learning alliance should involve stakeholders in the horizontal landscape, but also in the vertical value chain and in the governance structures of Fairtrade International. The incentives for participation of stakeholders in a learning alliance cannot be assumed, however, and much would rest on the ability of Fairtrade to act upon key findings and insights.

Conclusions

In this paper we have explained how impact assessment has developed in the field of Fairtrade covering studies commissioned by Fairtrade organizations and those by donors. Greater attention has been paid to impact assessment in Fairtrade, reflecting the picture in international development more widely. But the increased pressure for rigour in impact assessment, interpreted as experimental and quasi-experimental methods, presents some challenges for Fairtrade in the light of its inherent complexity and its wide scope of implementation, and given the importance of achieving utility. Utility is about ensuring that Fairtrade impact studies are useful to key stakeholders, with findings communicated to and acted upon by the wider organization, and also, critically, involving farmers and workers. There is scope to improve rigour, and not only through the use of counterfactual logics, as explained in this paper, but the challenge is to try to improve both rigour and utility. There are trade-offs between accountability and learning objectives in evaluation studies which are hard to avoid, but in this paper we have sought to provide some suggestions for how to achieve this. We have explained that rigour is about matching evaluation questions to impact design in the light of the specific attributes of the programme being studied and organizational ethos. It should not be conflated only with experimental and quasi-experimental designs. Other types of causality and theory-based evaluation can be employed, or combined. Mixed methods are also desirable, but we note the resource implications. Any resources invested in evaluation need to be proportionate to the scale of investment in the intervention (in this case Fairtrade). As Fairtrade is an approach seeking to achieve sustainable trade it is also important that it does not overly rely on donor funds. It is appropriate that donor funds be channelled into establishing better institutional learning systems and accountability mechanisms to help ensure that claims and achievements are consistent and credible, and support improvement and rethinking of strategies and assumptions where necessary.

While rigour can be improved it is also important that researchers do not over-claim from small numbers of case studies, and more systematic comparative analysis between cases is needed. Not all studies can or should be 'first-generation' type studies seeking to inform policy with robust evidence (which is difficult enough anyway). It is appropriate that all sustainability standard systems, including Fairtrade, also pay attention to the realities of fieldwork and to organizational ethos – if sustainability includes producer empowerment then it is important that the utility of an impact study is given full consideration. This includes ensuring that Fairtrade organizations take up the findings as far as possible and find ways that producers and workers can have their voices heard more directly than in the past. Facilitation of learning alliances at the sub-regional level would be one way of doing this.

About the authors

Valerie Nelson is Principal Researcher and **Adrienne Martin** is Head of Programme Development at the Natural Resources Institute, University of Greenwich, UK.

Acknowledgement

This chapter draws upon various research studies, including a major study funded by the UK Department for International Development on the poverty impact of sustainability standards.

References

Beach, D. and Pedersen, R.B. (2013) *Process Tracing Methods: Foundations and Guidelines*, Ann Arbor, MI: The University of Michigan Press.

Befani, B. (2012) *Models of Causality and Causal Inference* [online] Department for International Development (DfID) <http://betterevaluation.org/resources/guide/causality_and_causal_inference> [accessed 1 February 2014].

Blackman, A. and Rivera, J. (2010) 'The evidence base for environmental and socio-economic impacts of "sustainable" certification', Discussion Paper, Washington, DC: Resources for the Future.

Chambers, R. (2009) 'So that the poor count more: using participatory methods for impact evaluation', *Journal of Development Effectiveness* 1(3): 243–6.

Earl, S., Carden, F. and Smutylo, T. (2001) *Outcome Mapping: Building Learning and Reflection into Development Programs*, Ottawa, Canada: International Development Research Centre.

Edward, P. and Tallontire, A.M. (2009) 'Business and development: towards re-politicisation', *Journal of International Development* 21(6): 819–33.

Estrella, M. (ed.) with Blauert, J., Campilan, D., Gaventa, J. Gonsalves, J., Guijt, I., Johnson, D. and Ricafort, R. (2000) *Issues and Experiences in Participatory Monitoring and Evaluation*, Rugby, UK: Intermediate Technology Publications.

Eyben, R. (2013) *Uncovering the Politics of 'Evidence' and 'Results': a Framing Paper for Development Practitioners* [pdf] bigpushforward.net <http://bigpushforward.net/wp-content/uploads/2011/01/Uncovering-the-Politics-of-Evidence-and-Results-by-Rosalind-Eyben.pdf> [accessed 18 December 2013].

Garbarino, S. and Holland, J. (2009) *Quantitative and Qualitative Methods in Impact Evaluation and Measuring Results* [pdf] Governance and Social Development Resource Centre, Discussion Paper, University of Birmingham, UK <http://epapers.bham.ac.uk/646/1/eirs4.pdf> [accessed 18 December 2013].

George, A.L. and Bennett, A. (2005) *Case Studies and Theory Development in the Social Sciences*, Cambridge, MA: MIT Press.

Guijt, I., Arevalo, M. and Saladores, K. (1998) *Participatory Monitoring and Evaluation: Tracking Change Together*, PLA Notes Issue 31, pp. 28–36, London: IIED.

Holland, J. (ed.) (2013) *Who Counts? The Power of Participatory Statistics*, Rugby, UK: Practical Action Publishing.

International Trade Centre (ITC) (2011) *The Impacts of Private Standards on Producers in Developing Countries*, Literature Review Series on the Impacts of Private Standards; Part II (Doc. No. MAR-11-201.E), Geneva: ITC.

Jaffee, D. (2007) *Brewing Justice: Fair Trade Coffee, Sustainability, and Survival*, Berkeley, CA: University of California Press.

Kissinger, G., Brasser, A. and Gross, L. (2013) *Reducing Risk: Landscape Approaches to Sustainable Sourcing*, Scoping Study [pdf] Washington, DC: Landscapes for People, Food and Nature Initiative <http://landscapes.ecoagriculture.org/documents/files/reducing_risk_synthesis_report.pdf> [accessed 19 December 2013].

Laroche, K., Jimenez, R. and Nelson, V. (2014) *Assessing the Impact of Fairtrade in Peruvian Cocoa*, study commissioned by Fairtrade International, Chatham, UK: NRI.

Mayne, J. (2008) *Contribution Analysis: An Approach to Exploring Cause and Effect* [pdf] Institutional Learning and Change Brief No. 7 <www.cgiar-ilac.org/files/publications/briefs/ILAC_Brief16_Contribution_Analysis.pdf> [accessed 1 February 2014].

Murray, D., Raynolds, L. and Taylor, P. (2003) *One Cup at a Time: Poverty Alleviation and Fairtrade in Latin America*, Fort Collins, CO: Fairtrade Research Group, Colorado State University.

Neilson, J. and Pritchard, B. (2009) *Value Chain Struggles: Institutions and Governance in the Plantation Districts of South India*, Chichester, UK: Wiley-Blackwell.

Nelson, V. and Galvez, M. (2000) *Assessing the Social Impact of Ethical and Conventional Cocoa in Ecuador*, NRI report, Chatham, UK: University of Greenwich.

Nelson, V. and Martin, A. (2011) 'Impact evaluation of social and environmental voluntary standard systems (SEVSS): using theories of change', NRI Working Paper [pdf], Chatham, UK: University of Greenwich <www.nri.org/projects/tradestandards/docs/final_dfid_paper_on_using_theories_of_change_in_ie_of_standards.pdf> [accessed 5 February 2014].

Nelson, V. and Martin, A. (2012) 'The impact of Fairtrade: evidence, shaping factors, and future pathways', *Food Chain* 2(1): 42–63 <http://dx.doi.org/10.3362/2046-1887.2012.005>.

Nelson, V. and Martin, A. (2013a) *Final Technical Report: Assessing the Poverty Impact of Sustainability Standards* [pdf] Chatham, UK: Natural Resources Institute <www.nri.org/images/documents/project_websites/Assessing-PovertyImpacts/AssessingThePovertyImpactOfSustainabilityStandards.pdf> [accessed 1 February 2014].

Nelson, V. and Martin, A. (2013b) *The Strategic Use of Case Studies by Standard Systems*, NRI Working Paper, Chatham: UK, Natural Resources Institute.

Nelson, V. and Pound, B. (2009) *The Last Ten Years: A Comprehensive Assessment of the Impact of Fairtrade*, NRI Report, Chatham, UK: Natural Resources Institute.

Nelson, V. and Smith, S. (2011) *Fairtrade Cotton: Assessing Impact in Mali, Senegal, Cameroon and India: Main Report* [pdf], Chatham, UK: NRI <www.nri.org/projects/fairtradecotton/docs/Impact%20of%20Fairtrade%20Cotton%20-%20main%20report%20-%20final%20Apr2012.pdf> [accessed 5 February 2014].

Nelson, V., Tallontire, A. and Collinson, C. (2002) 'Assessing the potential of ethical trade schemes for forest dependent people: comparative experiences from Peru and Ecuador', *International Forestry Review* 4: 99–110 <http://dx.doi.org/10.1505/IFOR.4.2.99.17440>.

Natural Resources and Ethical Trade Programme (NRET) (1999) 'Ethical trade and rural livelihoods', in *Sustainable Rural Livelihoods: What Difference Can We Make?*, London: DFID.

Orr, A. (2013) 'Why were so many social scientists wrong about the Green Revolution? Learning from Bangladesh', *The Journal of Development Studies* 48(11): 1565–86 <http://dx.doi.org/10.1080/00220388.2012.663905>.

Oxfam (2013) *Process Tracing: Draft Protocol* [online] <http://policy-practice.oxfam.org.uk/blog/2013/02/~/media/C396B507E01C47AB-880D7EEF9ECCD171.ashx>.

Patton, M.Q. (2008) *Utilisation-Focused Evaluation*, 4th edn, London: Sage.

Pawson, R. and Tilley, N. (1997) *Realistic Evaluation*, London: Sage Publications.

Ragin, C.C. (1987) *The Comparative Method: Moving beyond Qualitative and Quantitative Strategies*, Berkeley, CA: University of California Press.

Ramalingam, B. (2008) 'Evaluation and the science of complexity'. Presented at the Evaluating Complexity Conference, NORAD, 29–30 May.

Ramalingam, B. (2011) *Learning How to Learn: Eight Lessons for Impact Assessment that Make a Difference*, Background Note, London: ODI.

Ramalingam, B. (2013) *Aid on the Edge of Chaos: Rethinking International Cooperation in a Complex World*, Oxford, UK: Oxford University Press.

Riddell, R. (2007) *Does Foreign Aid Really Work?* Oxford, UK: Oxford University Press.

Roberts, S., Robins, N. and Abbot, J. (1999) *Who Benefits? A Social Assessment of Environmentally-Driven Trade*, London: IIED.

Roche, C. (1999) *Impact Assessment for Development Agencies: Learning to Value Change*, Oxford, UK: Oxfam Publications.

Ronchi, L. (2002a) *The Impact of Fairtrade on Producers and their Organisations: A Case Study with COOCAFÉ in Costa Rica*, PRUS working paper, No. 11 [pdf], Poverty Research Unit, University of Sussex <www.sussex.ac.uk/Units/PRU/wps/wp11.pdf> [accessed 5 February 2014].

Ronchi, L. (2002b) *Monitoring Impact of Fairtrade Initiatives: A Case Study of Kuapa Kokoo and the Day Chocolate Company* [pdf] London, UK: TWIN <http://portals.wi.wur.nl/files/docs/ppme/TwinMEKuapaandDayA_5version.pdf> [accessed 5 February 2014].

Ruben, P., Fort, R. and Zuniga, G. (2008) *Final Report. Fairtrade Programme Evaluation: Impact Assessment of Fairtrade Programs for Coffee and Bananas in Peru, Costa Rica and Ghana*, study assignment by Solidaridad Coordinated by the Centre for International Development Issues (CIDIN), The Netherlands: Radboud University Nijmegen.

Solidaridad (2012) *The Solidaridad Network 2012 Annual Report* [pdf] Netherlands: Solidaridad <http://solidaridadnetwork.org/sites/solidaridadnetwork.org/files/The%20Solidaridad%20network%202012%20annual%20report.pdf> [accessed 5 February 2014].

Stern, E., Stame, N., Mayne, J., Forss, K., Davies, R. and Befani, B. (2012) *Broadening the Range of Designs and Methods for Impact Evaluations* [pdf], Working Paper 38, April 2012, report of a study commissioned by DFID, London: DFID <https://www.gov.uk/government/uploads/system/uploads/attachment_data/file/67427/design-method-impact-eval.pdf> [accessed 5 February 2014].

SustainAbility (2011) 'Signed, sealed, delivered: behind certifications and beyond labels', London and Washington, DC: SustainAbility <www.sustainability.com/library/signed-sealed-delivered-1#.UrLWGImYbIU> [accessed 19 December 2013].

Tallontire, A., Nelson, V., Dixon, J. and Benton, T. (2012) *A Review of the Literature and Knowledge of Standards and Certification Systems in Agricultural Production and Farming*, NRI Working Paper no 2, Chatham, UK: Natural Resources Institute.

Twin (2012) *Making International Supply Chains Work for Smallholder Farmers: A Comparative Study of Six Fair Trade Value Chains* [pdf] London: Fairtrade Foundation <www.fairtrade.org.uk/includes/documents/cm_docs/2012/M/Making_international_supply_chains_work_for_smallholder%20farmers.pdf> [accessed 18 December 2013].

Unilever, Oxfam, IIED (2012) *Measuring Fairness in Supply Chain Relationships: Methodology Guide* [pdf] London: IIED <http://pubs.iied.org/pdfs/16042IIED.pdf> [accessed 18 December 2013].

Vorley, B., Cotula, L. and Chan, M.K. (2013) *Tipping the Balance: Policies to Shape Agricultural Investments and Markets in Favour of Small-Scale Farmers*, research report, December 2013, London: IIED; Oxford: Oxfam.

Woolcock, M., Rao, V. and Bamberger, M. (2010) 'Using mixed methods in monitoring and impact evaluation', *Policy Research Working Paper* 5242 [online], World Bank Poverty and Inequality Team <http://elibrary.worldbank.org/doi/book/10.1596/1813-9450-5245> [accessed 17 December 2013].

Yin, R.K. (2014) *Case Study Research: Design and Methods*, 5th edn, Thousand Oaks, CA: Sage Publications.

Website

3iE website <www.3ieimpact.org/> [accessed 10 December 2013].

CHAPTER 3

Why 'place' matters in the development and impacts of Fairtrade production

Cheryl Mcewan, Alex Hughes, David Bek and Zaitun Rosenberg

Abstract

This chapter examines the importance of place for the cultural and environmental dynamics shaping Fairtrade cooperatives. It draws on a case study of the Eksteenskuil Agricultural Cooperative (EAC) in South Africa's Northern Cape, which supplies Fairtrade raisins to Traidcraft plc, one of the UK's leading Fairtrade organizations. It examines how the histories and geographies of place continually challenge and redefine the meaning and effectiveness of Fairtrade. It concludes with a number of recommendations for both Fairtrade organizations in general and EAC/Traidcraft specifically.

Keywords: South Africa, Fairtrade, place, geography, history, Traidcraft

THIS CHAPTER CHALLENGES THE 'one size fits all' discourse, which until recently has dominated Fairtrade, and advances arguments for sensitizing Fairtrade to the specificities of particular places. This approach focuses on historical legacies, political and cultural identities, the significance of geography, and environmental risk, which combine to drive the dynamics of producer groups and cooperatives as they cope with specific, local challenges.

The chapter draws on a case study of the Eksteenskuil Agricultural Cooperative (EAC) in South Africa's Northern Cape, which supplies raisins to Traidcraft plc, one of the UK's leading Fairtrade organizations. It examines how the specificities of place continually challenge and redefine the meaning and effectiveness of Fairtrade. The South African context is particularly interesting owing to the ways in which national and local policies of empowerment inform and affect the workings of Fairtrade codes and standards. However, rather than allude to 'South African exceptionalism' (Kruger and du Toit, 2007: 213), we use this case to illustrate that *all* places have histories and geographies that need to be properly understood for Fairtrade to work effectively. The paper draws on research conducted between January 2010 and November 2012, which included three periods of fieldwork in Eksteenskuil and 72 interviews (mostly in Afrikaans and translated into English) with members and non-members of EAC. A further 10 interviews were conducted with commercial, NGO and government informants in South Africa, and seven with Traidcraft

http://dx.doi.org/10.3362/9781780449067.003

staff in the UK. The paper first outlines the history of the relationship between Traidcraft and EAC, before demonstrating the significance of place history in gauging the challenges facing specific producer communities. The next two sections explore cultural and political challenges and geographical challenges facing EAC, followed by some recommendations for both Fairtrade organizations in general and EAC/Traidcraft specifically.

Traidcraft and EAC

Traidcraft plc began sourcing raisins, used mainly in its popular cereal bars (the Geobar), from the Eksteenskuil Farmers Association (EFA) in 1995, which was FLO (Fairtrade International) certified in 2003. The Eksteenskuil Agricultural Cooperative (EAC), comprising 89 farmers, replaced the EFA in 2007 in response to requirements of FLO standards and as a means to strengthen the partnership between Traidcraft and Eksteenskuil producers. The shift in legal status to a cooperative was encouraged by Traidcraft because it fits with the concept of Fairtrade as a developmental model and was supported by EFA as a means by which it could consolidate member produce, subcontract processing and market finished products (Traidcraft Visit Report, Eksteenskuil Farmers Association/SAD, 06/11/2006). The Northern Cape is one of South Africa's most impoverished provinces and EAC members are considered historically disadvantaged. Eksteenskuil more broadly includes approximately 180 households and more than 1,200 people living across 21 islands, grouped for administrative purposes into three areas, North, Middle, and South Islands (SLC, 2010) (see Figure 3.1). The majority of residents self-define as 'coloured'.

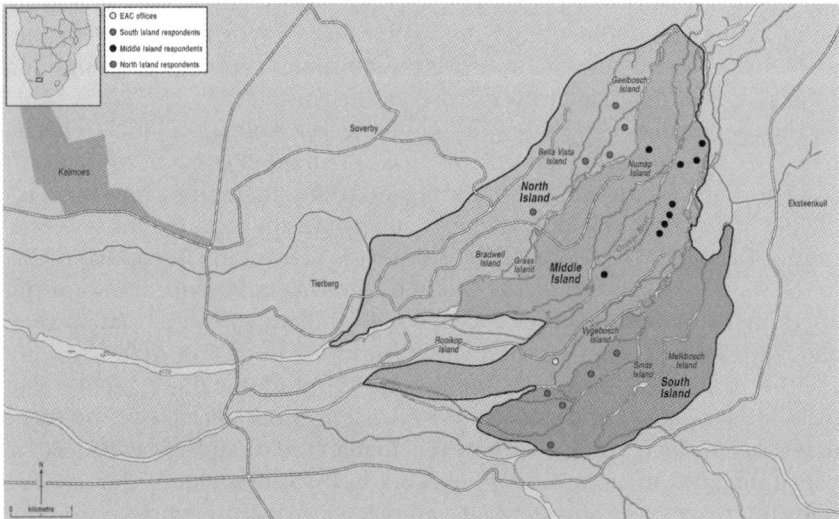

Figure 3.1 Eksteenskuil, near Keimoes, Northern Cape, South Africa

While this is an expression of identity, its origins are in the apartheid-era race classification legislation, the legacies of which still pervade official discourses and mindsets. As discussed below, this is one of the many factors that underpin EAC's complex external (and even internal) relationships. The current farming community of Eksteenskuil also includes several 'commercial' (defined as working more than 50 hectares) white farmers, landless labourers, and, during harvesting, migrant workers.

Of the 2,000 hectares of land in Eksteenskuil, 600 hectares are irrigation-fed arable farming. Raisins represent the main source of income, with lucerne, cotton, and vegetables also grown. The Orange River area is ideal for growing seedless grapes because of its semi-arid climate, very high summer temperatures up to 40 degrees Celsius, warm winter days and cooler nights. Its farmers produce some of the highest quality raisins in the world, specifically Thompsons raisins (late harvest, sun-dried grapes), Golden raisins (late harvest, wind-dried grapes), and Orange River Sultanas (early harvest, wind-dried grapes). EAC sells the majority of its raisins (400–600 tonnes per year, mainly Thompsons) to Traidcraft. Cooperative members sell their raisins primarily through the dominant local processor, South African Dried Fruits (SAD), which prior to the ending of apartheid held a monopoly on raisin exports and still has the second largest and the most modern fruit-processing plant in the world. The processors play a key role in the commodity chain since they grade the raisins delivered to them by EAC members as either Choice or Standard, which has an impact on price; they are also responsible for sorting and quality control, including pre-cleaning (removal of stalks, vacuuming, fumigation), washing and packing, quality inspection, and transporting, loading and shipping for export. Eksteenskuil farmers have had a relationship with SAD since the 1960s and, because it is now FLO-certified, it is the required processor for raisins supplied to Traidcraft. Despite this, some EAC members also sell to other processors (e.g. Red Sun) independently of the cooperative if they believe they will receive quicker payments. However, because other processors are not FLO-certified, these sales cannot count as Fairtrade and, therefore, do not earn premium monies. This bind to a single FLO-certified processor, which has caused some tensions between EAC and Traidcraft, was resolved to some extent in 2013, with EAC contracting Red Sun to do the processing rather than selling raisins to them, thus ensuring the raisins remain Fairtrade.

The principle of stable pricing structures does little in practice to benefit EAC farmers because for several years the Fairtrade minimum price (usually around £0.45 per kg) has been significantly lower than the market price (recently £1.13 per kg for Thompsons seedless raisins) (SLC, 2010). The key benefits of Fairtrade for EAC are, therefore, guaranteed access to markets via Traidcraft, a small price premium paid directly by SAD to farmers above the market price and the Fairtrade social premium. FLO stipulates that the social premium (£0.07 per kg), paid directly to the cooperative based on sales through SAD, should be used for community development at the discretion of EAC's elected board. To date, the premium has supported various projects, most significantly the purchase of farming equipment that can be hired at a minimal rental fee by members across the islands. However, despite these projects, our research (see also SKA, 2010) suggests that EAC underperforms as a cooperative, specifically in identifying developmental needs and the effective use of premium monies in meeting these needs, and that it faces challenges rooted, in part, in the history, geography, and cultural politics of the area. Little was known about these contexts when Traidcraft began its relationship with Eksteenskuil farmers. Fairtrade alone, while delivering some tangible benefits as discussed, cannot be expected to remedy many of the entrenched difficulties that the farmers continue to endure. However, as well as being reflected in impact assessments, we suggest that a deeper understanding of constraints rooted in historical, geographical, and cultural specificities would help Traidcraft, and Fairtrade organizations more generally, develop more effective systems of support for cooperatives.

Fairtrade and place history

Fairtrade production in South Africa has expanded rapidly since the ending of apartheid in 1994. Fairtrade organizations in the global North were keen to work with producer groups in post-apartheid South Africa, but often had little detailed knowledge or understanding of the histories and geographies of the communities with which they sought to work. One of the main challenges, and a consequence of the dispossession wrought under apartheid, was a relative dearth of smallholder communities from which to form cooperatives. Another challenge was the need to incorporate the more radical, but specific, South African understandings of 'fairness' into Fairtrade standards, including land reform and Black Economic Empowerment. While recent FLO initiatives have sought to adapt the Fairtrade standard to this South African context, this has mostly benefited the large number of commercial farms rather than the small group of cooperatives including EAC (see Kruger and du Toit, 2007; Hughes et al., forthcoming).

In contrast to smallholder communities elsewhere, Eksteenskuil was created via an apartheid-era resettlement scheme in accordance with the 1913 Land Act (Robins, 2001). Eksteenskuil was an Act 9 area from which a small number of white farmers were relocated during the late 1950s, to more productive areas elsewhere, and into which coloured people were relocated. Most Eksteenskuil families have lived there for three or four generations and are attempting to sustain livelihoods on land previously deemed non-viable for agriculture because of the flood risk. Moreover, while the small number of white farmers had held large areas of land, coloured farmers were limited to one hectare per family with the consequence that the majority of EAC farmers now farm plots of land that are fewer than 5 hectares (SLC, 2010). As discussed later, environmental risk presents considerable difficulties for maintaining sustainable livelihoods and the history and geography of Eksteenskuil presents challenges to creating an effective cooperative.

One of the difficulties for Traidcraft in empowering Eksteenskuil's farmers is the limits of Fairtrade in tackling the legacies of apartheid inequalities. This is illustrated by the constraints posed by the difficulties of land reform. As a historically disadvantaged group, EAC members are eligible for support from the government's Land Reform for Agricultural Development (LRAD) programme, which enables farmers to acquire land, and its land tenure reform programme, which enables farmers to obtain freehold titles for land owned (SLC, 2010). However, only six farmers have been successful in obtaining LRAD grants to purchase land and less than half of EAC members have received title deeds (SKA, 2010). Since FLO standards regarding land reform apply only to commercial estates with hired labour and not to cooperatives, Fairtrade does not play a role in alleviating this struggle.

Cultural and political challenges

One of the difficulties for Traidcraft has been establishing an effective and representative cooperative in the context of a membership in which capacity and confidence are either low or, because of geographical fragmentation, difficult to harness. A 2009 FLO audit, confirmed by our research, noted the dependence of EAC on the leadership of one individual, who for several years was both chair and general manager (he was recently de-selected as chair). In many ways, faith in the capacity of this individual, plus his force of personality, appear to have stultified the ability or willingness of other members to take EAC forward.

EAC's board has seven members, led by an elected chair, and it has representation from each of the three island groups. However, the FLO audit states that further work is needed on social and environmental development plans; according to Traidcraft:

> There is a big disconnect between what the co-op is doing and what the farmers are doing. ... I think its behaviours are distancing the membership. So in terms of becoming a co-op, it has to go out there and meet its members and actually begin that dialogue and start responding to its members' needs and actually start working to make sure that it functions as a co-op, that people are engaged with it. (Interview, Traidcraft supplier support team member, December 2010)

The new chair appears to be aware of these issues. However, in contrast to other Fairtrade cooperatives both in and beyond South Africa, EAC has engaged with very few projects that constitute explicit forms of community development. A significant proportion of the social premium funds the administration of EAC. It has not provided funds for schools, youth facilities, health clinics or community events, which have been highlighted as community needs by EAC members in a recent report (SKA, 2010). In part, this derives from EAC's preference to put money directly into programmes benefiting farmers economically, in particular the funding of training, providing rental equipment, and loans for planting new vines. This highlights a broader tension within cooperatives between business and development goals. As Burke (2010) argues, while pursuing business goals might generate material benefits for producers, it does not necessarily reduce the vulnerability and dependency of some producers, promote participatory development, or ameliorate discriminatory distinctions among cooperative members. According to the current EAC Chair, however, underperformance also results from farmers misunderstanding the cooperative:

> There is a need for training on how a cooperative works. It is almost a stigma that was carried from the old regime and that definitely needs to be changed with training, maybe focusing on the members and management to get rid of those stigmas and to see the benefits of being part of a co-op. (Interview, EAC Chair, Middle Island, February 2011)

This stigma arises from a specific historical context in which only white farmers were allowed to organize into cooperatives, which thus became part of the structures of apartheid domination (Ashton, 2011). EAC members, like many producers in the global South, have little understanding of Fairtrade generally (Getz and Shreck, 2006; Lyon, 2006; Kruger and du Toit, 2007), but are also confused about the role and workings of the cooperative that is intended to represent their interests.

In addition to these historical and cultural specificities that hamper the workings of the cooperative, interviews also reveal impediments to community relations connected to the strong ways in which farmers and their families identify culturally with the particular island groups. The island groups of North, Middle, and South present significant geographical anchors for the identities of farmers and their families, with Middle Island sitting at the administrative heart of Eksteenskuil (housing the EAC offices) and having relative wealth, status, and improved infrastructure (including the area's only paved road) in comparison with the more remote and generally poorer North and South Islands. An EAC administrator captures the relative wealth of Middle Island and her sense of how this is viewed by other island groups:

> Every island has got a different issue. Normally the North Islanders always say Middle Island is the rich farmers. I came here and we had a little house, just with a sink and with bowls, but in 2009 we got electricity after many years, so I mean if the North Island people say that we are rich, it is nonsense. (Interview, EAC Co-ordinator, Middle Island, March 2011)

From South Island, however, differentials in material wealth and administrative power are seen to be firmly connected to the continuing concentration of development opportunities on Middle Island and a failure of the cooperative to spread the benefits more widely:

> The paved road, things are happening on Middle Island, stuff is happening over there, nothing is happening on North Island. I'm not upset

about the road, but it is about the unfairness of how work was delegated, as all the people working on that were from Middle Island. The story was that when they were restoring their roads, then people on South Island would receive benefits, but instead it all went to Middle Island people.... People from Middle Island are now working on the bridges. The same people from the road are helping out with the bridges. Because they are close to the [EAC] office, they can go to the office and sort out their CVs, get them typed. By the time the contractor comes to the different islands, you don't have CVs ready, but there is a pile of CVs available at the office from Middle Island. (Interview, female farmer, South Island, March 2011)

While there are clear socio-economic gaps and cultural tensions between Middle and South Islands, the problems experienced and perceived on North Island are arguably most acute. A recent report, for example, reveals that unemployment rates are highest on North Island at just below 50 per cent (SKA, 2010). In addition, while most housing across Eksteenskuil is modest, made predominantly of brick with iron roofs and mostly without electricity, 'shack dwellings' (SLC, 2010), usually constructed out of reeds with corrugated iron roofs, appear more common on North Island. Gaps in material wealth are compounded by other issues. In particular, widespread alcohol problems (SKA, 2010) are believed by interviewees to be most problematic on North Island, with consequences for farmer participation in the cooperative:

Some of the farmers are too irresponsible because of alcohol abuse. In meetings people make promises and say they will cooperate. But they leave the meetings and don't follow up.... That's why you cannot depend on a lot of the farmers. It [alcohol abuse] is especially prevalent on North Island. Each island has its own little culture. There's a dark cloud hanging over North. (Interview, male farmer, North Island, September 2010)

Views about North Island moralities also affect the implement-hiring scheme. This began just before the EFA became a cooperative, with the purchase of three tractors and a wide range of farming equipment available for minimal rental fees to members on all three islands. The scheme is widely used and the majority of interviewees regard it both as a crucial element of their farming and as the main benefit of membership of EAC. However, for some farmers there are inevitable problems with the logistics of sharing a limited range of equipment:

The Co-op needs to be strict, not as lenient as in the past. The islands have their own little cultures. Everyone knows that people on Middle Island will take good care [of the implements], people on South Island will take good care, but people on North Island, forget it. *That* island. Things always come back broken. (Male farmer, Middle Island, September 2010)

The tensions between island groups also flared during the 2011 floods, which had devastating consequences for EAC members (discussed in more detail below). While the floods could not have been prevented, their severity could have been reduced by better planning, and EAC (and other organizations) was criticized by farmers, particularly on North and South Islands, for poor communication with them before, during, and after the floods.

The more severe infrastructural, agricultural, and social impacts of the floods were felt on North Island. For some of the larger farms, in particular those on Middle Island, the most significant problems were inaccessible areas of land, hiring seasonal labourers, and a reduction in raisin quality. In some of these cases, households had alternative income sources – often from lucerne, cotton or fruit and vegetable production – to cushion the blow (interviews with Middle Island farmers, March 2011). This contrasts with smaller farms in which whole families, solely dependent on raisins, were in many cases left with almost nothing and fighting for access to scarce resources. For landless and seasonal workers, the impacts of the floods on harvesting meant little or no work. Differences in flood damage impacts are also deepened by islanders' perceptions of each other's responses. While there were notable cases of farmers and landless workers helping each other, in particular with damage repairs on North Island, the responses of particular island groups were sometimes called into question:

> The way a lot of people handle stress is to sit and wait and feel very miserable and almost disempowered. We had an EAC Board meeting last week and we received a letter from South Island stating that they will not be able to cover any of their loans with the Co-op due to the flood and poor harvest this year. That letter already says 'I am helpless, I cannot do anything about this situation' instead of planning and thinking ahead and doing something and finding means to pay off your loan. (Interview, Middle Island farmer and EAC Board member, March 2011)

Tensions also emerged during an emergency meeting with the Department of Agriculture in March 2011 to conduct a survey of flood damage. Many North Islanders questioned the attendance of Middle Islanders, whom they felt had suffered far less destruction. Therefore, while EAC works to improve the livelihoods of its members against the backdrop of environmental challenges, as well as apartheid and colonial legacies, it does so in the context of a geographically and socio-economically divided Eksteenskuil community.

Compounding these problems, a significant weakness in the modus operandi of EAC, at least under the previous general manager, has been its negligible and ineffective relationships with external stakeholders. Interviews with the broader Eksteenskuil agricultural community and government officials (including Local Economic Development and Agricultural Extension Officers) reveal that opportunities to enhance raisin production or to diversify have been missed because of an inability to develop positive relationships with people in other organizations. This can be partly linked to the re-organization of local government. In the past there was a branch of local government in Eksteenskuil (based at the current EAC office); however, following the creation of the Kai !Garib District, the office was closed and all affairs are now managed via offices in Keimoes. Several respondents alluded to personality clashes at the individual level, but geographical isolation and lack of political visibility have also been significant. Factors that are deeply rooted in the history and culture of Eksteenskuil, such as the inward-looking attitudes of EAC Board members and paid officers and a sense of disconnection from the formal political system have continued to create difficulties for EAC in its relations with external stakeholders. The result has been that EAC has not engaged effectively with the municipality, local 'commercial' farmers groups, or the Department of Agriculture. Meanwhile, external stakeholders expect EAC to deliver beyond its remit. As one Northern Cape Municipality officer puts it:

> If you look at Eksteenskuil compared to other communities...we say is it really necessary for us to go and work there and there are other communities who are so unorganized? (Interview, Agricultural Extension Officer, March 2011)

There appears to be a sense, stated by several government officials, that because EAC exists the local community can be left to look after themselves.

Geographical challenges

There are two specific sets of challenges posed by the geography of Eksteenskuil, which present difficulties in meeting Fairtrade objectives concerning sustainable livelihoods and empowerment. The first is the environmental risk faced by farmers. South Africa is the world's second largest producer of raisins, with 70 per cent grown in the Orange River area. The Orange River is naturally prone to flooding and the frequency of catastrophic floods appears to be increasing (Knoesen et al., 2009). Situated on island braids in the river, Eksteenskuil is particularly at risk, yet this is not considered in Fairtrade impact assessments (e.g. SLC, 2010; SKA, 2010). 2011 witnessed the worst floods since 1988. The Orange River reached a height of more than 7 metres, with discharge levels of over 6,000 cubic metres per second in mid-January and again in early February. The second of the two flood peaks arrived at harvest time for Thompsons raisins with dramatic consequences. In some areas, whole fields were flooded, destroying vines completely or exposing their roots, thus increasing the risk of fungal root infections. Crucial infrastructure such as irrigation channels, electricity lines, dirt roads, and bridges suffered damage, particularly on North Island (Middle Island's new paved road remained intact). There were also significant consequences for raisin yields and quality, with the supply of highest quality grade raisins by EAC farmers reduced by 50 per cent to 200 tonnes. There are likely to be longer-term consequences for reduced yields because of damage to large areas of vines (see Figure 3.2). Furthermore,

Figure 3.2 Flood damage

20 per cent of the crop was sold to Red Sun because some farmers believed this would speed up grading decisions and payments at a time when cash flow was under extreme pressure. This reduced the Fairtrade premium for the 2011 harvest. Flooding also created illness, principally because for many the river provides the only source of fresh water, but also because mobile clinics were unable to access the islands. In an area of high prevalence of diseases such as diabetes, failure to access medicines compounded existing illness.

Traidcraft is faced with the paradox of attempting to support sustainable livelihoods in an area considered non-viable for agriculture because of environmental risk and in which these risks are becoming more frequent. Total rainfall and frequency of extreme weather events are predicted to increase over the Orange River basin over the next 30–40 years (Knoesen et al., 2009). In recent years, Traidcraft has needed to provide financial support to EAC farmers following damaging hailstorms (2002) and poor harvests (2005 and 2011). A further paradox, then, is that rather than empowering producers, some are at times heavily dependent on Traidcraft for sustaining their livelihoods. In addition, poor decisions were made by the previous EAC Board on the location of new vines, funded from premium monies, and levee maintenance. In some cases, new vines were planted adjacent to the river or in areas where levees had not been maintained and were entirely destroyed by the floods.

The environmental challenges faced by EAC are deepened further by the testing physical geography of Eksteenskuil. As the Supplier Support Coordinator at Traidcraft describes:

> The islands themselves are, although they are very close in terms of distance, in terms of actually access[ing] and getting around they seem to be very, very distant and that distance means that there tends to be quite a small amount of collaboration between the different islands and there is a sense of, between different islands, a sense of exclusion or resentment towards the Cooperative, just simply because of distance. (Interview, December 2010)

The EAC Board has attempted to meet the challenges by having group leaders on each of the islands. A male farmer interviewed on South Island explains this role:

> I...was a group leader, a supervisor, for South Island for a couple of years. My duties were pretty much as a messenger. If any notifications came from the [EAC] office, then I would have to go door-to-door to inform people. I also used to check their fields and see how they farmed and give advice. (Interview, February 2011)

However, the cooperative tends to rely on message boards and telephones as the key means of communication. The message boards are not particularly useful for a scattered community, only the better off farmers have landlines and, while many other farmers have access to mobile phones, they are very often unable to pay for airtime.

The geography of Eksteenskuil poses challenges to establishing participatory organizations that might more effectively identify and respond to community needs. For example, the EFA used to have a Women's Association that ran projects aimed at diversifying income streams, such as fruit gardens. However, this was discontinued because of logistical problems bringing women together from across the three islands. Yet 14 per cent of EAC's membership is women and, following a needs assessment report that recommended reviving a women's association (SKA, 2010), Traidcraft has supported a new Women's Forum. This attempts to bring together women from across Eksteenskuil to set up new projects and to provide business and administration training for EAC members and participants in the various projects, but geography again poses particular challenges:

> The distance is a problem. A multi-purpose centre on South Island is the only gathering place, but it does not make sense always. They usually say they will start at 2pm. They pick me up at 1pm and then pick up the other people and they start at 3.30pm. It is dark, half past six, seven o'clock when we come back after a meeting that was supposed to happen at 2pm. (Interview, female farmer, Middle Island, March 2011)

The meeting point has since been moved more centrally to the EAC office on Middle Island, but only at the suggestion of our project team, which points to some of the problems of agency within EAC. The physical landscape in which EAC operates clearly makes communication, inclusion, and cohesion incredibly difficult, particularly between the EAC Board and farmers across the island groups, but also between members of the cooperative more broadly.

Key recommendations

EAC faces continuing challenges regarding environmental risk and the need to foster community development along FLO lines in a locality where community cohesion is problematic. In this sense, EAC experiences similar difficulties of widening Fairtrade participation and engagement to those faced by many cooperatives around the world (Dolan, 2010a, 2010b; Lyon, 2006). The picture is not entirely bleak, however, and to make progress Traidcraft and the EAC Board might look towards building on some of the more positive elements of community life in Eksteenskuil. For example, there is evidence of friendship and support networks extending beyond island groups, revealed during the recent floods. For some interviewees, such networks provided a source of emotional support at challenging times. For the vast majority (97 per cent belong to a congregation; SKA, 2010), the church provides an important locus for this kind of support and could be used to better develop lines of communication between the EAC Board and its members. The Women's Forum, while achieving limited success and requiring attention from EAC and Traidcraft to improve participation, operates in a similar way to channel communication and foster support. As one Middle Island woman recounts in reference to the floods:

> I'm aware of how bridges collapsed on North Island and people not getting their raisins across the bridges. Even on South Island people could not get to the multi-purpose centre due to damage to bridges...The women [of the Women's Forum] actually contacted each other by phone and they informed each other. It was a good way, you are informed about their situation and you can relate to it. The conversations were good. (Interview, March 2011)

Such informal, inter-island networks provide an instructive model for EAC, which was accused of falling short in terms of maintaining contact with farmers at the time of the floods. Some interviewees suggest that EAC ought to decentralize to an extent and build sub-groups on each island, providing a mechanism for communication between the board and members.

In the aftermath of the floods and in response to FLO requirements regarding environmental development plans, it is clear that EAC needs to work towards developing a disaster management plan. When asked whether they would be willing to support such an initiative for EAC, the Regional Coordinator for Fairtrade Southern Africa replied:

> Yes, of course…We want resilient systems, as disasters will happen. We can say that in our future planning that we need to put these things in. We are trying to work more with [Fairtrade assessors/trainers] to share ideas and platforms. (Interview, February 2011)

In addition, North and South Islanders, expressing frustration with the continuing concentration of development opportunities on Middle Island, explain that there are many people on more remote islands with skills, training, and enthusiasm that could be applied to infrastructure projects and office tasks like book-keeping (interviews, August 2010 and March 2011). EAC could better harness these skills to develop greater attentiveness towards the challenges faced by farmers located in more remote areas of Eksteenskuil, and a communication system to increase their involvement. This attentiveness needs also to extend to the needs of Eksteenskuil's landless labourers, who are often marginalized by Fairtrade's emphasis on the smallholder farmer. However, there is also a case to be made that too much is expected of EAC, primarily because of the detached relationship with municipal government. EAC clearly cannot be expected to deliver the development needs of the entire Eksteenskuil area, but requires better relationships with external stakeholders, particularly various spheres of government.

Traidcraft has been limited in terms of its resources in fostering these relationships and their broader context. The Department of Agriculture has long been involved in development initiatives in Eksteenskuil; it was thus remarkable that one official had not heard of Traidcraft (interview, Department of Agriculture, March 2011). While resource constraints are difficult to surmount, better knowledge of the policy context and networks in which EAC is inserted, and the funding and extension opportunities that emerge from these, might allow Traidcraft to make a tangible contribution to the long-term development of Eksteenskuil. Such institutional mapping exercises could be useful tools within the broader Fairtrade movement, both for co-ops and external agencies such as Traidcraft.

Traidcraft might also see better returns on its engagement with more strategic planning and engagement. Encouraging EAC to form a stakeholder forum would deal with some of the issues discussed here. EAC itself could also have been more pro-active in this regard. A collaborative relationship with commercial farmers' groups, such as the Keimoes Farmers' and Orange River Associations, for example, would have enabled co-op members to receive regular flood-related updates and to report damage in 2011 (interview, Grape Manager at Keimoes export company and member of commercial Farmers' Association, December 2011). Thus, EAC's inward looking mindset, in part fuelled by mutual distrust between marginalized (largely coloured) and commercial (largely white) farmers, has reinforced the problems caused by their very real geographic isolation. A stakeholder forum might encourage a more outward-looking perspective that would reap economic dividends.

Finally, Fairtrade and other organizations might take a broader view of local economies. In the case of EAC, the narrow Fairtrade product focus is restrictive and increases the vulnerability of members to risk. Encouraging more diverse income streams is clearly a sensible option, and one to which Traidcraft has been amenable, for example through its encouragement of the Women's Forum in establishing small-scale fruit production. Along these lines, more could be done to encourage EAC members to develop the tourism potential of the islands, for example. While the landscape and cultural history create challenges for farmers, they also create potential to attract visitors to a grow-ing tourist destination in South Africa. And while it is not Traidcraft's remit to capacity-build in tourism, it could encourage better engagement between EAC and regional stakeholders in ways that might foster diversification. Unlike similar Fairtrade ventures, such as Thandi Wines in the Western Cape, the tourism potential of EAC has not been considered, not least because the 'Eks-teenskuil/Traidcraft Story' remains untold. Surprisingly, not even members of the EAC Board are aware that Eksteenskuil was the world's first Fairtrade raisin producer, or that there may be something of interest in this to visitors to the region.

Conclusion

It is fair to say that EAC has thus far struggled to fulfil its potential and that there is room for further community development and social transformation. In many ways the geography of Eksteenskuil is quite extraordinary. Farmers are prone to a series of hazards, particularly summer hailstorms and floods that regularly threaten their productivity. Their capacity to manage these haz-ards is severely reduced by the broader political-economic history, which has left many farmers with small, fragmented plots of land and no title deeds. Furthermore, a history of dispossession, discrimination, and disenfranchise-ment is a challenging context from which to build a confident community able to engage successfully with regional and international markets. Indeed, the notion of community, which is central to Fairtrade discourse, has to be challenged in this context as Eksteenskuil is more typified by divisions than a sense of collective endeavour. These divisions can be delineated in various ways, but are linked to the fact that Eksteenskuil was created by a relocation policy that brought together people from different places and backgrounds. Furthermore, the geography of the islands and the challenges this poses for communication and infrastructure development serve to deepen the sense of a lack of community.

For the past 18 months EAC has been at a crossroads. Changes in manage-ment and outlook have occurred putting the organization in a better place to move forward. However, the board and its staff face serious challenges includ-ing: a drop in demand from Traidcraft and difficulties in accessing markets for Fairtrade raisins elsewhere; variable yields, which make it difficult to secure long-term market contracts; reduced Fairtrade premium income and resources to deliver EAC's administrative roles; the heavy reliance on the voluntary efforts of board members; clarifying EAC's precise role, which is currently ambiguous in the eyes of many members; improving the organization's reputation as a project partner; and inculcating a sense of what it means to be a cooperative among the membership. On the positive side there is evidence that EAC's management has found new energy and vigour. There are participatory and social challenges for EAC in a context of chronic poverty, environmental risk, and a spatially fractured and culturally complex community. While Fairtrade has helped to provide a stable market for EAC members, it operates within a community already disadvantaged by both the legacies of apartheid and geography. In both Eksteenskuil and beyond, a deeper understanding of place – environmental risk (which climate change is increasing across the global South), the constraints and challenges of geography, and local identities and cultures rooted in specific histories – is critical to unravelling not only the impediments to community development, but also the possibilities.

About the authors

Cheryl McEwan is Professor of Human Geography, Department of Geography, Durham University.

Alex Hughes is Reader in Economic Geography, School of Geography, Politics and Sociology, Newcastle University.

David Bek is a Research Associate, School of Geography, Politics and Sociology, Newcastle University.

Zaitun Rosenberg is an independent researcher/trainer, Stellenbosch, Western Cape, South Africa.

Acknowledgements

The EAC case study is part of a wider research project entitled 'Ethical production in South Africa: Advancing a cultural economy approach'. We are grateful to the Leverhulme Trust (F/00128/BE) for funding this research. The funding source had no involvement in the study design, the collection, analysis and interpretation of data, preparation of the chapter writing the report, or in the decision to submit the chapter for publication. We would like to express our thanks to the participants in the research, especially to the staff at Traidcraft and members of the EAC Board, without whom the research would have been impossible. We thank also the many people involved in raisin production in Eksteenskuil who gave freely of their time, and Chris Orton of the Cartography Unit, Geography Department, Durham University, for producing the map. We are grateful to two anonymous referees for their constructive and helpful comments on the paper.

References

Ashton, G. (2011) 'Co-operatives for Development' [website], South African Civil Society Information Service <http://sacsis.org.za/site/article/608.1> [accessed 24 July 2013].

Burke, B. (2010) 'Cooperatives for "fair globalization"? Indigenous people, cooperatives, and corporate social responsibility', *Latin American Perspectives* 37: 30–52 <http://dx.doi.org/10.1177/0094582X10382098>.

Dolan, C. (2010a) 'Virtual moralities: the mainstreaming of Fairtrade in Kenya tea fields', *Geoforum* 41: 33–43 <http://dx.doi.org/10.1016/j.geoforum.2009.01.002>.

Dolan, C. (2010b) 'Fractured ties: the business of development in Kenyan fair trade tea', in S. Lyon and M. Moberg (eds.), *Fair Trade and Social Justice: Global Ethnographies*, pp. 147–75, New York: New York University Press.

Getz, C. and Shreck, A. (2006) 'What organic and Fair Trade labels do not tell us: towards a place-based understanding of certification', *International Journal of Consumer Studies* 30: 490–501 <http://dx.doi.org/10.1111/j.1470-6431.2006.00533.x>.

Hughes, A., McEwan, C., Bek, D. and Rosenberg, Z. (forthcoming) 'Embedding Fairtrade in South Africa: global production networks, national initiatives and localized challenges in the Northern Cape', *Competition and Change*.

Knoesen, D., Schulze, R., Pringle, C., Summerton, M., Dickens, C. and Kunz, R. (2009) *Water for the Future: Impacts of Climate Change for Water Resources on the Orange-Senqu River Basin*, Report to NeWater, Pietermaritzburg, South Africa: Institute of Natural Resources.

Kruger, S. and du Toit, A. (2007) 'Reconstructing fairness: fair trade conventions and worker empowerment in South African horticulture', in L. Raynolds, D. Murray and J. Wilkinson (eds.), *Fair Trade: The Challenges of Transforming Globalization*, pp. 200–19, London: Routledge.

Lyon, S. (2006) 'Evaluating fair trade consumption: politics, defetishization and producer participation', *International Journal of Consumer Studies* 30: 452–64 <http://dx.doi.org/10.1111/j.1470-6431.2006.00530.x>.

Robins, S. (2001) 'NGOs, "Bushmen" and double vision: the ≠Khomani San land claim and the cultural politics of "community" and "development" in the Kalahari', *Journal of Southern African Studies* 27: 833–53 <http://dx.doi.org/10.1080/03057070120090763>.

SKA (Sandra Kruger & Associates) (2010) *Eksteenskuil Agricultural Cooperative Land Use and Socio-Economic Survey*, Report compiled for SKA/Traidcraft, January 2010, Pniel, South Africa: SKA.

SLC (Sustainable Livelihood Consultants) (2010) *Impact Assessment of Fairtrade in South Africa: Case Study Report, Eksteenskuil Agricultural Cooperative*, 11 June 2010, Keimoes, South Africa: EAC.

CHAPTER 4

Partnerships in Fairtrade coffee: a close-up look at how buyers and NGOs build supply capacity in Nicaragua

Jason Donovan and Nigel Poole

Abstract

This chapter examines efforts by buyers and NGOs to build the supply of Fairtrade coffee from the Nicaragua-based cooperative Soppexcca following the coffee crisis. Support was aimed at transforming Soppexcca into a viable business, able to respond to the needs of its coffee-farming members. Results show that Soppexcca made significant gains, including expansion of infrastructure, growth in membership, and increased financial stability. However, important issues remained, related to democratic governance, future growth and stability, and the provision of services. Results suggest that advances in building cooperatives do not easily translate into increased capacities at the household level. While some important gains were detected, in general, producers struggled to intensify coffee production and take full advantage of their access to preferential markets. This chapter makes a plea for deeper discussions about how buyers and NGOs can more effectively contribute to building the supply of high-quality Fairtrade coffee, and the need for increased coordination and mutual learning as part of the process.

Keywords: Fairtrade, coffee, smallholders, cooperatives, development practice, Nicaragua

FAIRTRADE COFFEE IS A BIG BUSINESS, the growth of which shows no sign of slowing down. In 2010, approximately 88,000 tonnes of Fairtrade coffee were consumed globally – nearly a threefold increase since 2005 (FLO, 2011). In the United States, consumption of Fairtrade coffee increased by 50 per cent each year during the 10-year period ending in 2010 (Transfair, 2010). In the United Kingdom, Fairtrade accounts for roughly 25 per cent of the roast and ground market by value, with more than 120 companies licensed to market (Fairtrade Foundation, 2012). Fairtrade coffee is offered in major supermarkets throughout Europe and North America, and includes some of the largest corporate players in the coffee sector. The demand for Fairtrade stems, in part, from consumers' concerns over social and environmental issues in the global economy. With its rise in popularity, as well as increased competition

http://dx.doi.org/10.3362/9781780449067.004

from other sustainability labels, many buyers and retailers have emphasized high quality to differentiate themselves in an increasingly crowded market segment.

Fairtrade structures how Northern-based coffee buyers interact with cooperatives and their members in producing countries. At a minimum, buyers agree to provide cooperatives with guaranteed prices and an additional payment for locally defined projects. In many cases, however, deeper buyer–cooperative relationships evolve within the Fairtrade framework, reflecting shared values and organizational commonalities, as well as buyers' need to increase access to high-quality coffee (Raynolds, 2009). Such partnerships may feature security in contracting, pre-financing, technical assistance, additional price premiums for quality, and joint strategy formulation. In Nicaragua, for example, well-established Fairtrade cooperatives and a US buyer joined forces to build cupping laboratories for assessing coffee quality before export and to organize an umbrella organization that promoted high-quality certified coffee at the national level (Bacon, 2013). Given the risks involved, buyers are more likely to invest in partnerships with more established cooperatives with professional management.

Cooperatives are positioned in the chain between Northern-based coffee buyers and smallholder coffee producers. They maintain a portfolio of coffee buyers and establish links with Fairtrade support organizations, as well as seek out partnerships with development organizations. In Nicaragua, where the state has limited presence in the coffee sector, cooperatives also play an important role in supporting their members in the expansion and intensification of high-quality coffee production. In their efforts to grow into viable businesses, cooperatives often seek to build their infrastructure, professionalize their management, and increase their technical capacities in coffee production and processing. NGOs and other development organizations have invested considerable resources in the promotion of coffee cooperatives in Latin America and elsewhere. There is a general assumption that strong cooperatives are well-positioned to support their members in the sustainable intensification of coffee production (e.g. by providing technical assistance, credit, and production inputs), and thus contribute to poverty and conservation goals. Such support to coffee cooperatives formed a major element of donor strategies for addressing the coffee crisis (1999–2005) in Central America (Varangis et al., 2003).

This chapter explores how buyers and NGOs in the international coffee chain supported the Nicaragua-based cooperative Soppexcca in its effort to source high-quality coffee from smallholder coffee producers. Soppexcca was organized in 1997 and, at the time of data collection, had about 500 members. Soppexcca's membership more than doubled during the early years of the coffee crisis, as coffee producers sought higher coffee prices. In addition to providing access to certified markets, Soppexcca offers annual credit for coffee production, multiyear credit for strategic coffee-related investments, and technical assistance. In 2009, all of Soppexcca's coffee exports were Fairtrade certified. In relation to Soppexcca, we examine:

- how buyer investments and NGO interventions contributed to Soppexcca's overall development and its ability to engage in long-term chain partnerships; and
- how Soppexcca, with buyer and NGO support, contributed to building the capacity of its members to deliver high-quality coffee.

Case study context

Buyer interactions with Soppexcca's predecessor cooperative, Jiprocoop, in the late 1990s played a critical role in the organization of Soppexcca and the formation of its management structure. In 1997, after five years exporting Fairtrade coffee, Jiprocoop declared that it would not be able to meet its contractual obligations for the delivery of green coffee. During the previous year, Jiprocoop had received US$640,000 in 'pre-financing' from six buyers (approximately 60 per cent of the value of the contracts). However, poor oversight of the cooperative's administration permitted theft of the pre-financing by the cooperative's manager and the export committee (Denaux, 2008). Without the pre-financing, Jiprocoop was unable to purchase coffee from its members and thus was unable to repay the pre-financing. Jiprocoop was declared insolvent in 1997.

Five of the six European debt-holding coffee buyers offered a solution for repaying the debt. A new corporate entity would be created which would hold the debt of the defunct Jiprocoop, with which the buyers would continue to trade. This offered the prospects of recovering the losses incurred by mismanagement, ensuring supplies of the high-quality coffee, and at the same time supporting a development agenda around smallholder coffee production. Thus was created Soppexcca in 1997, a firm in which the buyers would have a strong management hand, constituted as a 'corporation'. The corporate structure enabled efficient and professional governance in the interests of shareholders first rather than other stakeholders such as the coffee growers.

Soppexcca and its members gradually repaid its debt obligations and expanded commercial relations with coffee buyers in the United States. In 2004 the buyer/owners allowed Soppexcca to reorganize itself as a cooperative with producer-members' interests paramount, but retaining the professional management. The reversion to the cooperative form post-recovery reflected a desire to return the organization to the hands of the member-stakeholders, to benefit from the tax-free status offered to cooperatives, and to receive increased support from development organizations. At the time of data collection, various European and US coffee buyers continued to provide no-interest credit to Soppexcca for the purchase of coffee from its members.

NGO interventions also played an important role in the development of Soppexcca's supply base. Between 2000 and 2009, Soppexcca received financial and technical support from NGOs and donors totalling roughly $2 m from nine NGOs and projects. In several cases, multiple interventions were carried out by the same NGO. Support aimed to build a credit programme (including multiyear credit for coffee rejuvenation and expanding production areas), provide humanitarian assistance, expand infrastructure and equipment, and finance technical assistance by Soppexcca.

Methods

Data collection and analysis focused on assessing the productive capacity of Soppexcca and its members, and the role of NGO and buyer partnerships in helping to build their capacity. Key informant interviews, household surveys, and secondary information were used to assess capacities and changes in capacities following an intense period of interventions by NGOs and buyers. The assessment covers the period between 2004 and 2008. In some cases, a shorter timeframe was used, for example a three-year period was used for reporting purchases of fertilizer (recognizing the limitations of recall for more routine purchases). In reporting coffee production and sales, the period was extended to 2009 to capture production that was sold in early 2009.

At the cooperative level, we assessed: 1) governance structures; 2) administrative capacity; and 3) financial viability. At the household level, we assessed: 1) productive base (area under coffee; access to fertilizers, as a proxy for soil fertility; and investments in tools, equipment and machinery); 2) coffee production practices; and 3) credit access and income flows. Quantitative and qualitative data were collected to determine these changes, while mainly qualitative information was used to understand their relevance and the underlying reasons.

Data collection at the cooperative level relied upon key informant interviews and the collection of secondary information. The Soppexcca staff interviewed included the directors of management, extension, and credit, and members of the board of directors. Staff members were consulted on various occasions during the data collection period. In addition, interviews were carried out with Soppexcca's buyers, local coffee buyers, NGO supporters, and certification agencies. Soppexcca supplied information on membership, coffee exports, credit provision, relations with buyers, and overall business strategy. Information provided by Soppexcca was triangulated with its members during household interviews (see below).

At the household level, 292 coffee-producing households were interviewed (about 95 per cent of the membership of 11 of Soppexcca's 18 base cooperatives); 32 per cent (n=71) of the sampled households were certified organic. Insights into attribution were gained by asking respondents the extent to which they considered that changes were attributable to engagement with Soppexcca. In other cases, attribution insights were gained by singling out the most probable causes of the change from various potential causes. It was not possible to identify the effects of any one intervention or partnership on local capacities, thus attribution refers to the set of interventions and interactions that were channelled through Soppexcca.

Understanding the factors behind variation in outcomes among households constituted an important element of this study. Households were clustered according to: 1) area under coffee production in the 2008–2009 coffee-growing year; and 2) percentage of total household income derived from off-farm sources in 2008. A three-cluster solution emerged from this analysis, with household livelihood descriptors and cluster characterization as follows:

- *Diversified small-scale farmers (DSF)* (n=77). Relatively small area under coffee production; high dependence on income derived from off-farm labour activities (often as wage labour for other, usually larger, farmers); some contribution from other crops.
- *Specialized small-scale farmers (SSF)* (n=162). Relatively small area under coffee production; majority of income derived on-farm from coffee, with contributions from banana, citrus, beans and other products.
- *Specialized large-scale farmers (SLF)* (n=53). Relatively large area under coffee production; majority of income derived from coffee, with contributions from livestock, banana, citrus and other products.

Unless otherwise indicated, coffee quantities are presented as pre-dried parchment coffee: the state of coffee when it is sold by producers to buyers such as Soppexcca (45 kg of export green coffee are commonly processed from roughly 90 kg of pre-dried parchment coffee produced by farmers in north-central Nicaragua).

Results

Outcomes for Soppexcca

Governance structures. In 2004, Soppexcca changed from a corporation to a cooperative and its elected board of directors met for the first time. Evidence during the assessment period indicates that the board faced major challenges in effective governance. One reason was insufficient skills in business and financial administration, combined with limited access to information. A former board president noted that he received no prior training in basic business or in cooperative management. What skills and knowledge he acquired while on the board came from trial and error. A similar experience was reported by a former member of the Oversight Committee – the committee that reviews the financial operations of the cooperative. Informants noted that the board and the Oversight Committee generally did not have access to timely financial information, largely because of a lack of information rather than inaccessibility of information. Interviews highlighted the board's reluctance to question, debate or probe Soppexcca's management regarding strategic decisions and investments. According to one former board member, 'Any effort to discuss the decentralization of Soppexcca's administration drew criticism from the other board members because it was perceived to show a lack of respect for [the professional manager].' It is worth mentioning that no evidence was found to suggest that Soppexcca's management thwarted greater inclusion of members in cooperative governance. Rather, our findings suggest that greater inclusion was not a priority.

Administrative and marketing capacities. Soppexcca benefited from strong managerial capacities prior to the period. A professional manager held the cooperative together during the worst of the coffee crisis, negotiating new contracts with buyers and obtaining NGO assistance. Interviews with buyers highlighted the ability of Soppexcca's management to build relations based on trust and mutual respect. According to one buyer, 'We feel a special trust with Soppexcca. They kept paying off the debt even though they didn't have to.' Trust was reflected in tangible ways. For example, in 2009, when Soppexcca announced its difficulty capturing its members' coffee due to high levels of local competition during the harvest season, interviewed buyers agreed to adjust their price formula so that prices offered by Soppexcca were more competitive with local farm-gate prices. Another buyer noted that 'if Soppexcca has to request an adjustment in their price, then there is always a good and transparent reason'. During interviews with buyers, concern was expressed over the high level of dependence on the manager for most business functions. However, neither buyers nor Soppexcca's NGO partners seemed aware of the limited participation of members in Soppexcca's governance.

Prior to the assessment period, Soppexcca enjoyed strong ties with coffee buyers, NGOs, and its membership base. During the period, Soppexcca forged new ties with US coffee buyers, while maintaining the strong relations that existed previously. The 2008–2009 harvest was sold to seven buyers: five from Europe purchased 59 per cent of the total volume exported and two from the United States purchased the remaining 41 per cent. The five European buyers had purchased about the same amount from Soppexcca every year since 1999. US buyers began to purchase coffee from Soppexcca in significant volumes beginning with the 2004 harvest. None of the interviewed buyers reported major problems with Soppexcca related to the quality of coffee delivered or compliance with contractual terms (including repayment of pre-financing). One buyer regarded Soppexcca as the most reliable among the 10 cooperatives in Latin America from which it purchased coffee.

Physical assets and income flows. Prior to the period, Soppexcca's physical capital was basic, consisting mainly of an office and warehouse space. By the end of the period, Soppexcca's stock had grown to include a dry-coffee processing plant, 11 offices for base cooperatives, a plant for the production of chicken manure fertilizer, two coffee houses, and a cupping lab. Purchase of the dry-coffee processing plant required long-term loans, grants, and the expenditure of cooperative earnings. The plant, which began operations in 2010, is expected to provide increased control of the production process (improved quality) and an additional income stream for Soppexcca, thus offering an option for reduced dependence on donor support in the future. The fertilizer plant was not in operation during the period due to uncertainties regarding the use of chicken manure from large-scale commercial broiler farms in organic coffee production. The newly constructed offices for base cooperatives offer the potential for greater consolidation of Soppexcca's base cooperatives, which have yet to play a major role in the delivery of Soppexcca's services (e.g. credit, technical assistance) or in taking the initiative to offer additional services (e.g. transportation, collective purchase of inputs).

Soppexcca's yearly income flows vary considerably based on negotiated prices and production volumes. Table 4.1 shows Soppexcca's estimated income after paying growers and export and processing expenses between 2005 and 2008. Data on costs for operating Soppexcca's administration were not available. However, the data in Table 4.1 shows that relatively little was available for covering salaries and capital investments. Key informant interviews with Soppexcca staff confirmed that project funds covered much of Soppexcca's administration costs and strategic investments. Given the recent major investments in the dry-processing mill, it is unlikely that, in the mid-term, Soppexcca will be able to operate without continued subsidies from NGOs and projects. That said, an efficient dry-processing mill has the potential to reduce export and processing expenses and to open a new income source (for example, provide milling services to other growers/cooperatives). Its extension and credit programmes remain dependent on grants.

Soppexcca began and ended the period with a relatively high level of debt. However, during the period, it proved its capacity to repay debt and build trust with creditors. Soppexcca began the assessment period with a debt to coffee buyers of nearly $500,000 and limited working capital or investment capacity. During the period, the cooperative repaid its debt from funds obtained from the export of coffee and with contributions from members (in the form of forgone social premiums). Shortly after doing so, however, it accumulated $280,000 in new debt for the purchase of the dry-coffee processing plant. On an annual basis, Soppexcca received loans from buyers and Fairtrade lending

Table 4.1 Income and expenses (US$) from Fairtrade coffee sales by Soppexcca, 2005–2008

	Total sales (45 kg green coffee)	Weighted average price	Total income	Purchase of coffee from growers	Export and processing expenses	Income after grower, export, and processing expenses
2005	12,242	118.5	1,450,026	1,224,200	140,538	85,288
2006	9,594	133.2	1,277,760	1,160,840	110,136	6,784
2007	5,935	136.1	807,770	718,135	68,134	21,501
2008	10,155	159.5	1,619,340	1,320,150	116,579	182,611

Source: authors' calculations, based on data provided by Soppexcca

organizations, totalling roughly $700,000 in 2009, which allowed Soppexcca to cover advance payment to its members for coffee delivery.

Outcomes for Soppexcca's members

Productive base. The total area under coffee production increased by nearly 30 per cent between 2004 and 2008, from 570 ha to 736 ha (Figure 4.1). The highest change was recorded by households from the SSF cluster (31 per cent), although changes only slightly smaller were recorded for households from the other clusters. Household interviews identified a mix of factors that allowed expansion of the coffee area, which typically included multiyear credit from Soppexcca. For households in the DSF and SSF clusters, growth in the area under coffee production likely reflected efforts to revive coffee area lost during the coffee crisis (due to neglect or removal for the planting of basic grains).

An understanding of the local context provides insights into why households from the DSF were the least likely to build their natural capital endowments, despite the expansion of Soppexcca's services and improved conditions for coffee marketing. For members of two base cooperatives, which together made up nearly 33 per cent of the DSF cluster, a history of struggle to obtain, manage, and retain their collectively owned coffee plantations impeded investments in natural capital. In one case, internal divisions among community members over how to produce and market the coffee for their collectively owned plantation resulted in 13 years of limited investment in coffee production. In 2003, individual land titles were obtained, with the help of Soppexcca. In another case, households linked through the collective ownership of a former state-owned plantation incurred approximately $80,000 in debt during the late 2000s for legal fees to fight off conflicting claims to their land. Until the debt is paid in full, the land title is being held in the custody of the legal representation.

The ability of households to make efficient use of their land under coffee production depends, in part, on their timely access to quality fertilizers.

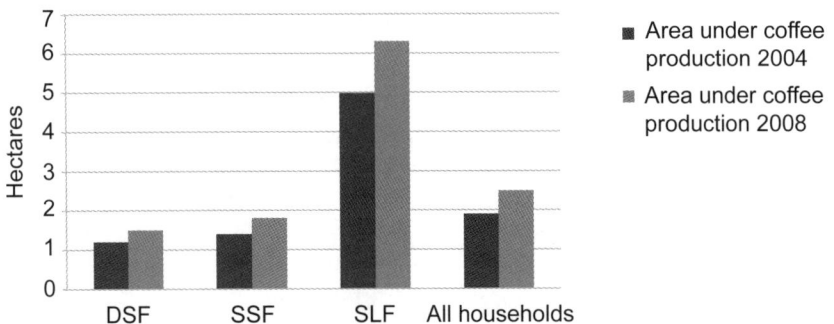

Figure 4.1 Change in area under coffee production between 2004 and 2008, by cluster

Coffee production mines nutrients from the soil, which, if not replaced through organic or inorganic fertilizers, results in gradually declining productivity (Van der Vossen, 2005). The average coffee yield in Nicaragua is 1,383 kg/ha (Flores et al., 2002). Evidence from long-term experiments in Nicaragua suggests that shade-grown organic and conventional coffee production in the country can reach productivity levels of 1,487 kg/ha and 1,927 kg/ha, respectively, with moderate levels of fertilization (Haggar et al., 2011). However, the average productivity for the sampled organic and conventional producers, at 726 kg/ha and 1,278 kg/ha, fell below these estimates. Among households in the DSF cluster, results were more discouraging, at 552 kg/ha for organic producers and 582 kg/ha for conventional producers. This suggests that lack of access to fertilizers remains a barrier to sustaining natural capital.

Among households producing conventional coffee, the relatively high costs of inorganic fertilizer presented a challenge to replenishing soil nutrients lost to coffee production among cash-strapped producers. Data on inorganic fertilizer use (complete and urea) were collected from 152 households; 22 households, or 14 per cent of those sampled, reported no purchase of inorganic fertilizer during the 3-year period between the 2005 and 2008 coffee growing years. Among DSF households, approximately 42 per cent applied at least one 45-kg bag of complete fertilizer in the 2008–2009 coffee growing year, while 18 per cent applied at least one bag of urea. The number of DSF households that applied inorganic fertilizer and urea is significantly higher in 2008 than for the previous two years. Despite the overall increase in fertilizer application, however, most households in the DSF cluster did not reach the estimated nitrogen threshold (39 kg of nitrogen/ha) for achieving reasonable productivity levels. Households identified short-term credit from coffee buyers as the main factor contributing to fertilizer purchases.

Improvements in infrastructure at the household level played a major role in Soppexcca's strategy for improving coffee quality. Physical capital for wet milling includes the construction/refurbishment of mill enclosures, construction/refurbishment of fermenting tanks or the purchase/repair of machines for depulping and pumping water. The average investment by households in the DSF cluster was $198 during the four-year period, skewed upward by a few households; among the 72 households in the cluster, only 12 (17 per cent) reported cash investments for improved wet milling (Figure 4.2). Investments by SSF, while significantly higher than those of the DSF cluster, remained low at $593. Moreover, 70 SSF households, or nearly half the cluster, reported no cash investments during the period. Investments by SLF households, at nearly three times those of SSF households, showed considerably less variation within the cluster. Credit by Soppexcca contributed $97,847 to investments in wet milling infrastructure and machinery, or roughly 48 per cent of total reported household expenditure.

Households also reported acquisitions of machinery, tools, and infrastructure for agricultural production, in addition to those used for wet milling

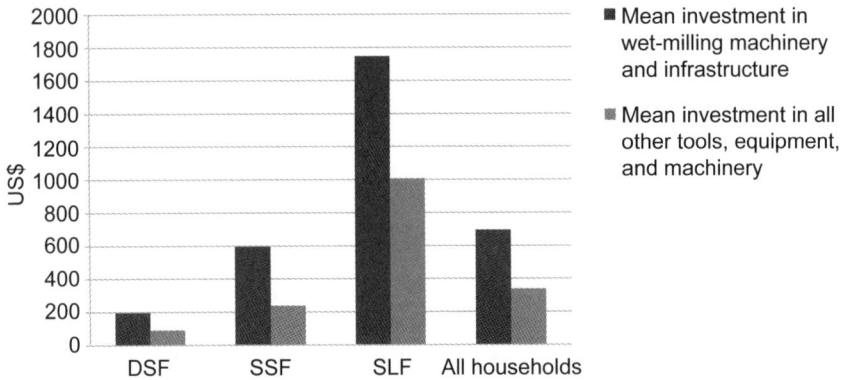

Figure 4.2 Purchase of tools, equipment, and machinery, 2004 to 2008

during the four-year period between 2004 and 2008. The extremely low investment by households in the DSF cluster stands out, at $91 (Figure 4.2); investments they made were generally confined to basic tools for production of coffee and basic grains. Similar to experiences in the building of physical capital for wet milling, households in the SSF cluster achieved higher investments than their DSF counterparts, but the absolute level of investments was low. In general, findings suggest that households from DSF and SSF clusters struggled to build their physical capital endowments for farm production compared with investments by SLF households, which included relatively large purchases of mechanized machinery for the production of coffee, livestock, and off-farm business activities.

Production practices. Implementation of good practices for coffee was an important focus of Soppexcca's technical assistance. Results were mixed. On one hand, most households increased their skills for reducing environmental contamination and providing higher-quality coffee. For example, the majority of households reported the application for the first time of select coffee harvesting during the period (54 per cent), as well as the use of environmentally friendly techniques for dealing with wastewater from wet milling (66 per cent). However, circumstantial evidence suggested that skills for proper plantation management, including the pruning of coffee bushes and shade trees, which play an important role in determining coffee productivity, disease resistance, and overall soil health, changed relatively little in response to Soppexcca-provided technical assistance.

Traditionally smallholders in Nicaragua do not practise regular pruning or other forms of improved crop management on their coffee plantations. Soppexcca aimed to facilitate the modernization of members' crop management through its training and technical assistance programme. However, according to Soppexcca staff, efforts to encourage more intensive tree management for coffee production have been frustrated by: 1) a general reluctance by producers to trim or stump coffee trees that are productive; and 2) the limited ability of Soppexcca staff to engage intensively with producers for upgrading their crop management skills (interview R.R., 24 November 2009). Not mentioned, but likely a major contributing factor to the limited uptake of improved crop management, are the potentially high trade-offs involved in shifting labour and other resources to coffee production from other livelihood activities (see Stoian et al., 2012, for a discussion in the context of value chain development).

A basic condition for modernizing coffee management is the development of the required skills. As the only provider of technical assistance for most of the households, Soppexcca had an important role to play in this respect. Households reported their perceptions on the utility of technical assistance for coffee production between 2007 and 2008: 44 percent (n=129) of the households reported being dissatisfied or highly dissatisfied with technical assistance provision. Household responses shed light on the nature of the problem:

- 'We were visited once in 2008, but the extensionist didn't provide technical advice; he arrived to inform us of a meeting at the cooperative'.
- 'I lack advice when I need it: on one occasion I requested a visit from the extensionist because the coffee berries were falling off the branches, but he never came'.
- 'Visits are only for estimating the harvest – the extensionist does not know my coffee plantation. He sends others from the community to assist me and does not provide advice'.
- 'Sometimes he indicated which product I should use, but the extensionist did not indicate the doses and I burned the plants'.

There is little doubt that the design and implementation of an effective technical assistance programme aimed at resource-poor farmers is a complex undertaking. Soppexcca's assistance programme was relatively young at the time of data collection and fully dependent on external funding. Over time, Soppexcca is likely to strengthen its capacity to deliver more effective services. This may involve a deeper understanding of the needs of different types of farmers, better diagnostic and decision-making tools, as well as a greater coordination within Soppexcca (i.e. linking technical assistance with credit).

Credit access and income flows. Most households (57 per cent) reported no access to short-term credit prior to joining Soppexcca. During the assessment period, opportunities for obtaining short-term credit increased, in part due to linkages with Soppexcca, with only 12 per cent of sampled households reporting no access to credit. Among households that received short-term credit, most (n=160, 55 per cent) reported Soppexcca as their only source of credit.

Other credit sources included specialized lending organizations, coffee buyers, NGOs, and, to a lesser extent, informal lenders and commercial banks. Collateral requirements varied. While the terms offered by Soppexcca were relatively favourable, the average amount provided was small. For example, in the 2007–2008 coffee growing year, the mean annual credit amount for DSF households was $197, with $390 for SSF households, and $1,805 for SLF households. Even for households with relatively small coffee holdings, Soppexcca-provided credit is unlikely to cover variable production costs, much less facilitate more strategic investments in asset building.

Before discussing income benefits from Fairtrade coffee sales, a brief discussion of 'side-selling' is warranted (i.e. the diversion of sales from formal to informal channels). In general, Soppexcca members have price and other incentives to sell their first-quality coffee to Soppexcca. Given that Soppexcca purchases only first-quality coffee, it is logical that members will sell their second-quality coffee (10–15 per cent of total harvest) to local buyers. However, results suggest that members divert a significant amount of first-quality coffee to buyers other than Soppexcca. For organically certified households, the mean percentage of coffee sold to Soppexcca between 2008 and 2009 was 73 per cent, while for conventional producers, the mean percentage was 57 per cent (Figure 4.3). Across all the clusters, the most common response was insufficient liquidity to cover production expenses for harvest (n=31). This is especially true for the SLF households, which tended to purchase more inputs and rely on hired labour. In addition, households from one community mentioned the importance of strong relationships with a local buyer, who provided technical assistance and credit. In other cases, especially within the DSF and SSF clusters, households identified emergencies, household expenses,

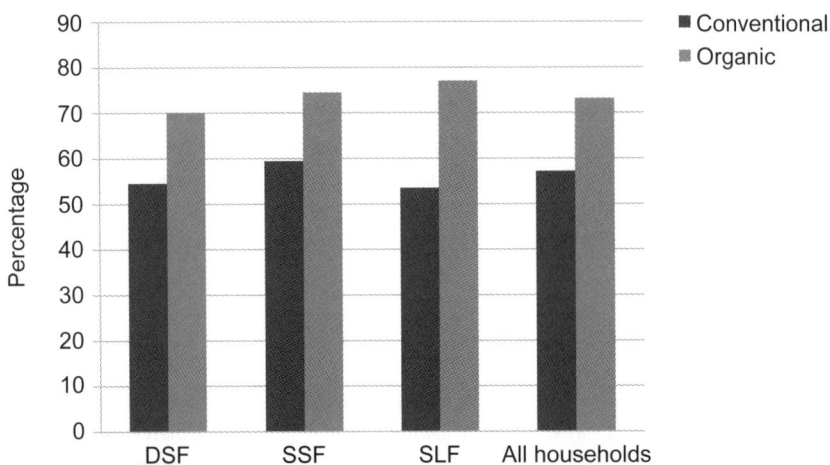

Figure 4.3 Percentage of coffee sold to Soppexcca, by producer type and cluster (2-year average, 2008 to 2009)

and strong quality requirements as the main reason for selling to other buyers. The following quotes from households in the DSF and SSF clusters highlight these points:

- 'Low production and lack of money affect our ability to send our children to classes in the first months of the year'.
- 'Our production was low. Had we delivered the production to Soppexcca, we would not have received any income because of our existing debt with Soppexcca'.
- 'The final payment is very late, and we need to pay coffee pickers; also, it has happened that our coffee has been too humid to pass inspection by Soppexcca'.
- 'Mr Gutierrez pays better than Soppexcca; Soppexcca has too many price deductions, and Mr Gutierrez is less concerned with quality'.

Table 4.2 presents estimates of the income benefit for Soppexcca members from coffee sales, taking into account sales to Soppexcca and to other buyers and allowing for the differences in farm-gate prices between coffee buyers. Among households from DSF and SSF clusters that produced conventional coffee, the actual income benefits from participation in Soppexcca were small, at $39/year and $102/year, respectively. Income benefits would have been

Table 4.2 Estimated annual income benefit from Fairtrade coffee sales (2-year average, 2008 to 2009)

Cluster	Average total coffee production (45 kg sack green coffee)	Potential income if all coffee sold to Soppexcca[1]	Potential income benefit if all coffee sold to Soppexcca[2]	Actual income, taking into account sales to other buyers	Actual income benefit from sales to Soppexcca	% of potential income benefit captured
Conventional						
DSF	5.9	643	71	611	39	55
SSF	18.0	1,962	216	1,875	129	60
SLF	100.2	10,922	1,202	10,363	643	54
Total	*31.3*	*3,412*	*376*	*3,251*	*215*	*57*
Organic						
DSF	6.6	898	257	821	102	39
SSF	9.5	1,292	371	1,198	163	44
SLF	49.4	6,718	1,927	6,275	890	46
Total	*14.0*	*1,904*	*546*	*1,758*	*232*	*42*

[1] The following two-year average farm-gate prices (2008 to 2009) were offered by Soppexcca: $136/45-kg sack for organic coffee and $109/45-kg sack for conventional coffee.

[2] Difference in income generated from all coffee production being sold to Soppexcca versus income generated from all coffee being sold to other buyers. A farm-gate price of $97/45-kg sack was used for estimating income from sales to other buyers. This price is 75% of the 2-year average (2008 to 2009) of the average New York 'C' contract price between December and March – the period during which farmers in Nicaragua sell their coffee.

more than twice the actual benefits if households had sold all of their production to Soppexcca. Organically certified households from the DSF and SSF clusters experienced higher income benefits than their conventional counterparts, at $102/year and $163/year, respectively. However, these households also struggled to maximize their income benefits from participation in formal markets. On average, organically certified households captured only 42 per cent of the total possible income benefits due to selling coffee to other buyers.

Conclusions

Buyers in the coffee chain played a vital role during the initial stages of Soppexcca's development, and continued to play an important role in Soppexcca's operations during the assessment period (e.g. through the provision of pre-financing and willingness to negotiate prices above Fairtrade floor price). The sourcing of high-quality coffee motivated their investments and interactions with Soppexcca. Following the coffee crisis, NGOs stepped in to build local capacities for the production, processing, and marketing of high-quality coffee. Soppexcca's strong professional management – a lasting outcome of previous buyer interventions – made it a useful partner for NGOs looking to advance poverty reduction and environmental goals. Soppexcca is not alone in having received considerable NGO support: the literature highlights the high level of support given to some cooperatives in Latin America that participate in certified markets: for example, El Ceibo in Bolivia (Bebbington et al., 1996) and Forestcom in Guatemala (Nittler and Tschinkel, 2005).

Despite major gains during the assessment period, however, Soppexcca remained highly vulnerable to challenges in the local environment and to internal and external shocks. The vulnerability derived, in part, from Soppexcca's limited success in capturing more of its members' production, increasing its members' coffee productivity, and building stronger membership participation in cooperative governance. Soppexcca's coffee buyers made clear their concerns over Soppexcca's vulnerability to a change in management. However, both buyers and NGOs were reluctant to seek out dialogue with Soppexcca and its network of business and NGO supporters to address the complex problems faced for future growth and development. One could also imagine the reluctance of any one buyer or NGO to challenge Soppexcca (e.g. to decentralize decision-making or improve the performance of services), as buyers and NGOs also depended heavily on Soppexcca for providing high-quality coffee and the implementation of programmes that were expected to contribute to development goals.

Results at the household level showed that Soppexcca, with NGO and buyer support, provided important services to its members which otherwise would not have been available. Evidence suggests that Soppexcca's technical assistance and credit programmes played an important role in households' ability to improve the quality of their coffee production, expand their area under coffee production (and rejuvenate existing areas), and reduce their vulnerability to asset erosion and food insecurity (e.g. through higher prices and access to credit). However, many households struggled to intensify coffee management and benefit from the higher prices offered by Soppexcca. In some cases, annual credit was used to meet household consumption needs, rather than to intensify coffee production. In other cases, the institutional context was highly unfavourable to coffee intensification (e.g. the lack of livelihood security and weak community organization). The poorest households, which tended to depend heavily on off-farm income, were the least able to benefit from their participation in the value chain. In general, evidence suggests that households faced major trade-offs in investing their scarce assets in coffee production. These findings echo those of other recent studies in Nicaragua (e.g. Wilson, 2010; Beuchelt and Zeller, 2011).

This study highlights some of the complex challenges and dilemmas facing cooperatives in building long-term commercial relations with Fairtrade coffee buyers and advancing goals related to poverty reduction and the environment. With their focus on building a reliable source of high-quality coffee from Nicaragua, buyers showed a willingness and ability to advance cooperative development. However, buyer interactions with Soppexcca were not enough to generate the local capacity development that was needed to build a sustainable supply base. NGOs showed greater interest in building local capacities, but were unwilling to question the design of their interventions or engage Soppexcca in order to build more inclusive governance or more effective services. NGOs and projects operated largely independent of one another, although they often shared similar goals and operated under tight deadlines and stretched budgets. Looking forward, the building of sustainable supplies of high-quality, Fairtrade coffee will require greater coordination and collaboration among chain stakeholders, including buyers, NGOs, researchers, and certification systems, particularly with a view to reaching an adequate level of appropriate investments in individual and organizational capacities. As a starting point, discussions will address the short- and long-term needs and circumstances of cooperatives and their members, as well as the role of different stakeholders in the development process. Building a culture of collaboration will take time and dedication, but doing so may very well be essential for encouraging the innovation, risk-taking, and shared learning needed to build supply capacity in less time and with fewer resources.

About the authors

Jason Donovan is a Marketing Specialist at the World Agroforestry Centre, Lima, Peru.

Nigel Poole is the Associate Dean for Learning and Teaching at the School of Oriental and African Studies, London.

References

Bacon, C. (2013) 'Quality revolutions, solidarity networks, and sustainability innovations: following fairtrade coffee from Nicaragua to California', *Journal of Political Ecology* 20: 98–115.

Bebbington, A., Quisbert, J. and Trujillo, G. (1996) 'Technology and rural development strategies in a small farmer organization: lessons from Bolivia for rural policy and practice', *Public Administration and Development* 16: 195–213.

Beuchelt, T. and Zeller, M. (2011) 'Profits and poverty: certifications troubled link for Nicaragua's organic and fairtrade coffee producers', *Ecological Economics* 70: 1306–24 <http://dx.doi.org/10.1016/j.ecolecon.2011.01.005>.

Denaux, G. (2008) *Lo Veo y No lo Creo: La Historia de 11 Años de la UCA Soppexcca*, Nicaragua: Jinotega.

Fairtrade Foundation (2012) *Fairtrade and Coffee: Commodity Briefing* [pdf] <www.fairtrade.org.uk/includes/documents/cm_docs/2012/F/FT_Coffee_Report_May2012.pdf> [accessed 24 January 2014].

Fairtrade International (FLO) (2011) *Challenge and Opportunity: Supplement to Annual Review 2010–11*, Bonn, Germany: Fairtrade International.

Flores, M., Bratescu, A., Martínez, J.O., Oviedo, J.A. and Acosta, A. (2002) *Centroamérica: El impacto de la caída de los precios del café*, Mexico City: CEPAL.

Haggar, J., Barrios, M., Bolaños, M., Merlo, M., Moraga, P., Munguia, R., Ponce, A., Romero, S., Soto, G., Staver, C. and Virginio, E. de MF (2011) 'Coffee agroecosystem performance under full sun, shade, conventional, and organic management regimes in Central America', *Agroforestry Systems* 82: 285–301 <http://dx.doi.org/10.1007/s10457-011-9392-5>.

Nittler, J. and Tschinkel, H. (2005) *Community forest management in the Maya Biosphere Reserve of Guatemala. Protection through Profits*. Report for the United States Agency for International Development (USAID) and the Sustainable Agriculture and Natural Resource Management (SANREM) Collaborative Research Support Program (CRSP), University of Georgia.

Raynolds, L. (2009) 'Mainstreaming fair trade coffee: from partnership to traceability', *World Development* 37(6): 1083–93 <http://dx.doi.org/10.1016/j.worlddev.2008.10.001>.

Stoian, D., Donovan, J., Fisk, J. and Muldoon, M. (2012) 'Value chain development for rural poverty reduction: a reality check and a warning', *Enterprise Development and Microfinance* 23(1): 54–69.

Transfair USA (2010) *Fair trade certified coffee: Impact report* [website] <http://fairtradeusa.org/resources/impact-reports> [accessed 24 January 2014].

Utting-Chamorro, K. (2005) 'Does fair trade make a difference? The case of small coffee producers in Nicaragua', *Development in Practice* 15(3/4): 584–99.

Van der Vossen, H. (2005) 'A critical analysis of the agronomic and economic sustainability of organic coffee production', *Experimental Agriculture* 41(4): 449–73 <http://dx.doi.org/10.1017/S0014479705002863>.

Varangis, P., Siegel, P., Giovannucci, D. and Lewin, B. (2003) *Dealing with the coffee crisis in Central America: Impacts and strategies*, World Bank Policy Research Working Paper 2993, Washington, DC: World Bank.

Wilson, R. (2010) 'Indebted to fairtrade? Coffee and crisis in Nicaragua', *Geoforum* 41: 84–92 <http://dx.doi.org/10.1016/j.geoforum.2009.06.008>.

CHAPTER 5

Enhancing Fairtrade for women workers on plantations: insights from Kenyan agriculture

Muhaimina Said-Allsopp and Anne Tallontire

Abstract

The growth in the market for Fairtrade certified agricultural exports from Africa has been rapid, promising empowerment for workers and communities through the Fairtrade Premium. Increasingly the Joint Bodies that administer the premium and the kinds of projects funded have been the subject of mounting criticism. Drawing from two empirical studies on Kenyan flowers and tea that explored pathways to empowerment for women workers on plantations, this chapter compares and contrasts the practices of two standards mechanisms operating on the farms: the Joint Body (JB) and the Gender Committee (GC). This analysis finds that the GCs were more empowering for women workers than the JBs and draws out examples of good practice from the former that could help to improve practice in Fairtrade in plantation agriculture. The chapter argues that appropriate training for members and non-members of committees alike, organizational and spatial structures, the nature of representation, and mechanisms for strengthening voice are of great importance in ensuring empowering outcomes for workers.

Keywords: Fairtrade, gender, agriculture, empowerment, women, Kenya

As the fairtrade standard has become increasingly important in both the floriculture and tea sectors in Kenya, increasingly, concerns have been raised with respect to the impacts of Fairtrade on workers (particularly women) (Nelson and Martin, 2012; Tallontire and Said-Allsopp, 2013). More specifically, questions have been raised about whether the Joint Body (JB) is adequate to deliver Fairtrade International's (FLO) core objective of hired labour standards; that is, the empowerment of workers rather than minimum worker rights (FLO, 2010: 12). In this paper we consider how in practice the JB could become more empowering, especially for women workers. We draw on two related studies of Kenyan agriculture which sought to understand worker experiences of plantation employment and the operation of standards and through this compare the workers' experience of Fairtrade through the JB with Gender Committees (GCs) which were also established on the farms studied.

http://dx.doi.org/10.3362/9781780449067.005

A JB is instituted on Fairtrade certified farms under the 'hired labour' standard for Fairtrade. Its role is to receive and use the Fairtrade Premium (the 'extra' part of the Fairtrade price designated for the development of producers), which accrues to producers through trade. We acknowledge that the Fairtrade hired labour model does not solely hinge on the JB as a mechanism for empowerment; some aspects of the Fairtrade hired labour standard are linked to empowering effects through enhanced job security and promoting freedom of association. However, the JB is the most tangible mechanism, particularly for workers, and an aspect to which FLO has dedicated considerable attention.

The Kenya Flower Council (KFC) began to promote the use of 'Gender Committees' on Kenyan flower farms in the wake of labour rights campaigns in 2002–03. The chief executive officer of KFC says that they were instituted to enable women's voices to be heard in the auditing of the KFC code, because previously, she says, 'the women were shy to talk' (interview 20 May 2008). GCs play an important role in the audit process, facilitating interviews with female workers who represent the bulk of the workforce and providing a tool through which the gender-related recommendations from audits could be implemented and monitored. While the mechanism originated within floriculture, the tea company in our study, which also engages in floricultural production, has implemented the mechanism across its operations. Farm managers in Study A explained that they established gender committees to be a voice for women workers and to help them to fight against 'women's problems', particularly sexual harassment, which at the time was both widespread and prolific.

In this paper we compare these two committees and explore how they work, how they could be improved in order to deliver empowerment, particularly for women workers, and how the two committees could learn from each other.

Our analysis draws on interviews and focus groups with workers, farm managers, standard setters, and other industry spokespeople from two studies. Study A analysed empowerment within two (related) companies that supplied horticultural and tea products to the UK (Said-Allsopp, 2013). For contextual purposes, we also drew on the findings of a second related study (Study B) which investigated a wider sample of 11 floriculture firms in Kenya that were also involved in the same Kenya–UK value chain, in order to explore workers' understanding of social and environmental standards (Tallontire et al., 2011). The operation of standards was part of the wider context of the first study, but the second examined more explicitly how standards were being developed and applied in the value chain.

In Study A, women workers were interviewed in two phases and from two companies (Company A and Company B) that each had multiple farm sites. Phase I (2008) comprised 14 focus group discussions (FGDs) with 163 women workers in Nairobi (vegetables), Naivasha (flowers), and Kericho (flowers and tea), in which they were asked about the changes (at work and at home) that they had experienced during their employment, their aspirations for the future, and plans for achieving these. Phase II (2009) involved semi-structured interviews with 78 women workers which examined their experiences in more depth. The sample included general workers and supervisors as well as Gender Committee members.

In Study B there were 29 focus groups with both male and female workers on 11 flower farms. The sampling framework for farms was based on ensuring a range of experience with standards. The FGDs with workers were stratified by gender and production section (e.g. greenhouse or packhouse) and included some discussions with shop stewards.

The fieldwork from both studies highlighted that workers were more aware of Fairtrade than any other standard. Further, it was the one in which they felt most involved, largely because of the Fairtrade premiums and the Joint Body (JB). Nevertheless, knowledge of Fairtrade was limited to workers from only four firms, despite six of the firms in our collective sample being currently Fairtrade certified and another two expressing an interest in Fairtrade at the time of the fieldwork. The data on GCs relies on the in-depth research at the farms investigated in Study A.

Our approach to the comparative analysis of the two standards mechanisms is to examine how they operate on the ground, drawing on the perspectives of the actors using the standards mechanisms, rather than focusing on compliance with the requirements of the standards (Loconto, 2010; Ouma, 2010). We are interested in how the standards are embedded within the local context, including how different standards may become 'entangled' with each other and inform each other through practice (Aasprong et al., 2013). We explore worker perspectives and identify practices related to the standards, particularly what may be considered 'best practice' with respect to empowerment outcomes.

Our analysis of the workers' testimonies was largely an inductive process, through which we identified three areas as being crucial for women's empowerment through standard mechanisms: the gender composition of the committee; project selection and the processes surrounding this; and training and education. These areas of concern are analysed in turn with respect to each of the two standards mechanisms.

Fairtrade in Kenya

An important part of Fairtrade is Fairtrade International's hired labour model. FLO has two standards for Fairtrade, one focused on small producers and, our concern here, one for 'conditions of hired labour' pertaining to plantations or large-scale commercial agriculture. There are 168,000 workers involved in Fairtrade, predominantly in Africa and Asia. Fairtrade is the dominant model for some crops, such as flowers, and is important in tea. In 2012, 100 per cent of flowers and plants were under the hired labour model and workers accounted for 60 per cent of the combined workers and small producers involved in Fairtrade tea (FLO, 2012).

In Kenya, the Fairtrade standard has become increasingly important in the cut-flower sector. While some Kenyan flower farms were certified to Fairtrade standards before 2005, more farms were certified when the UK's Fairtrade Foundation began to issue licences for retailers to sell Fairtrade certified roses. Fairtrade flowers were first sold in the UK in March 2004 but Fairtrade certified flowers had been available in Switzerland through Max Havelaar since around 2000. By 2008, there were 20 FLO certified companies (18 producers and two traders) in Kenya. While Fairtrade was regarded as the benchmark standard for the sector by our interviewees, there are several standards in Kenyan floriculture, with growers certified according to membership of particular bodies (e.g. the Kenya Flower Council) or their target markets (e.g. German buyers may require the Flower Label Program or the Dutch auctions require Milieu Programma Sierteelt, MPS) (Riisgaard, 2009, 2011; Tallontire et al., 2005).

In the tea sector, Fairtrade certification has been sought after by certain brands and, particularly in the UK, retailers. However, growers are starting to engage with Rainforest Alliance certification, which is becoming a more widespread requirement as a result of commitments by major buyers such as Unilever (Ochieng et al., 2013). Many tea companies also follow the Ethical Tea Partnership's code of labour practice.

While standards proliferate throughout export agriculture, there is relatively limited understanding of the mechanisms by which impacts emerge (Nelson and Martin, 2012). It is clear, moreover, that impact is profoundly affected by context (Nelson and Pound, 2009; Center for Evaluation, 2012). Standards may be enacted in different ways and, in practice, they are embedded with local context which may affect their implementation practices, often leading to unintended outcomes (Loconto, 2010; Ouma, 2010; Fisher et al., 2013).

Comparison of practices in the Joint Body and Gender Committee

We discuss the practices of the JB and the GC on the farms studied in this section. Of course, these are not the only organizational structures on the farms concerned with worker affairs. Out of the 100,000 workers employed in the flower sector, an estimated 60 per cent are members of the Kenya Plantation and Agricultural Workers Union (KPAWU) (KHRC, 2012). NGOs have argued that the trade unions (TUs) are not doing their job in representing workers, especially female workers, and highlight a gulf between the high politics of the general secretary's office and under-resourced regional organizers (KHRC, 2012).

Other organizational structures such as welfare committees or even (at least for women) the TU were not seen by workers as spaces where they could exert their voice. For example, the welfare committees established by farm management with the remit of dealing with worker disputes were said to be 'on the side of the company. They get paid KSh200 [US$2.33] extra and the chair gets paid KSh500 [$5.82] extra, so they don't want to lose this. When a problem goes to them, they decide in favour of the company not the worker' (GC member and Supervisor, August 2009, farm B).

In a context where mixed gender groups such as TUs and welfare committees continue to be dominated by men, it is crucial from an empowerment perspective that women have a neutral space over which they have ownership, independent of men and the management. As shall be demonstrated below, the GCs provide such a space, and the JBs also have potential for worker voice to be heard but, as we show, there are some challenges in practice, especially for women workers.

Gender composition of the two committees

The Fairtrade hired labour standards indicate that the Joint Body comprises elected workers, and must be legally independent from the company, but there must also be representatives of the company on it, in addition to democratically elected worker representatives. This democratic aspect is crucial to the second objective of the JB: its link to empowerment, through the capacity building impacts of decision-making and project planning.

Fairtrade's strong ethos of gender equality means that the rules regarding the Joint Body highlight the need for equal representation of men and women on the JB (FLO, 2007a). However, it has proved tricky to ensure sufficient female participation on the JBs, as women have been reluctant to stand for election due to cultural norms.

Workers cite a lack of information and education as the problem; managers on farms and several key informants concur. However, a solution remains elusive. One option farms have pursued is to try to 'assist' committees to become more gender balanced. JB election processes have evolved so that, increasingly, workers are trained on the purpose of the JB, and in the words of an FLO official, how such representatives differ from TU officials. In some cases, seats on the committee may be reserved for women, but this is a very tricky balance to maintain: 'If you leave it too laissez faire – you can end up with it all men. But you cannot impose it … If you impose, it will come out that there were "not elections but selections". If you let it go, during the inspection they [FLO] will say that there is not enough women', a consultant supporting producers told us (interview 9 September 2008). Women's ability to perceive themselves as agents of change was limited; regardless of whether they propose ideas for projects that would benefit them during the consultation phase, the projects selected were not those they suggested, nor do they have any idea of how these decisions were reached. Women committee members as well as general workers frequently stated that projects were chosen by the men on the committee and they had not been able to influence the decision-making process.

At the time of the study, the GCs at Companies A and B were composed exclusively of women. The strength of the committee lay in the level of support they received from management as well as their clear mandate upon creation – to tackle sexual harassment. While a recent study (KHRC, 2012) found that some cases persist, interviews in both studies A and B found no instances of sexual harassment, a finding that workers attributed to the GC. GCs have been arguably the most important tool in the fight against sexual harassment of women workers on farms in Study A, both as a vehicle for disseminating education and training, as well as through sensitization of workers.

As sexual harassment was a crucial issue for companies, considerable power was put into the hands of the committee and any worker found guilty was summarily dismissed. By the time the issue had been dealt with, the power of 'wamama gender' (the Gender Mamas) had been cemented in the eyes of both male and female workers. 'The gender committee has been given responsibility, they are very highly respected here' said one woman worker. Interestingly, no additional prestige was accorded to GC chairs over members in the eyes of other workers; all were wamama gender.

Women workers had confidence in the GC as a forum where women could defend the rights of fellow women workers without being under the control of men: 'The gender committee is important because if a male worker does something to a female worker like sexual harassment, he is reported to the gender committee and the male worker will be answerable for his actions' (FGD, Company A). As neutral spaces which women have ownership of independent of men and the management, the GCs were able to effect far-reaching changes on a variety of issues that have evolved along with women's changing needs (e.g. developing from a body specifically tasked with dealing with sexual harassment issues, to organizing demonstrations at the community level, and establishing rotating savings and credit associations). While we would not argue for the JB to become an exclusively female domain, indeed in 2011 female GC members on some sites requested they be allowed to choose sympathetic males to join the committees in order to be able to better tackle *gender* issues, it is important for women's voices to be guaranteed within the JB so women do not continue to be the largely silent and marginalized members they were found to be.

Decision-making in the Joint Body and Gender Committee

Despite the great potential that Fairtrade has for contributing to women's empowerment, women workers in Study A who spoke of Fairtrade, all talked of how they had *previously* had high hopes that the premium money would change their lives. Much of the discussion of Fairtrade in the focus group discussions centred on the investments made through the premium fund. The JB and the premium projects (at least in theory) present opportunities for workers to build up their skills (e.g. short courses for workers to improve their skills, such as tailoring, IT, driving, carpentry) and to develop social infrastructure (a housing project; community water; construction of schools; a bus for hire), as well as to deal with more immediate welfare needs. There were a number of examples where premium funds had funded childcare facilities, which would meet the practical gender needs of women. At Company A, female workers told us 'there is a Fairtrade project [a day-care centre] here where children are provided with food, [disposable nappies] and clothes; all of which have been paid for by Fairtrade'.

However, the projects mentioned above were seen in only 4 of the 13 farms investigated in the two studies. Stories abound in Naivasha about how premium money has been spent on galvanized tin roofing sheets, Fairtrade branded baseball caps and T-Shirts, TV sets and aerials, and other similarly individualistic projects that fail to meet many of the ideals set out in the standard (FLO, 2007a). The majority of workers in Study A were under the impression, at least initially, that the premium would be distributed to workers as a form of a bonus. The result of people not understanding the purpose of the premium manifested itself in the sorts of projects that were then proposed.

Women workers often viewed the projects as being more beneficial for men than women. The skewed gender balance for beneficiaries of the skills training courses was corroborated by a consultant supporting producers who said that 'At [one flower farm] they asked for driving classes; there are 62 men and 4 women having lessons. This year we will talk to the women; some of them want to do hairdressing and tailoring', (interview 9 September 2008). When talking of these projects, one woman stated, 'We women feel like we have been left behind'. The gender bias in project selection can be linked, firstly, to a lack of transparency in how the JB operates on these farms and, secondly, to the dominance of men within these committees that means that women, who are constrained by cultural norms, bow to the wishes of male committee members. It was often the case on Company A's flower farm that projects of benefit to women were outvoted by the male majority. For example, a crèche using the premium funds was repeatedly vetoed by male committee members who felt that the project would benefit women not men. It was only when this project was rephrased as being a project for children and not their mothers, and using arguments surrounding child nutrition and care, that the project was finally approved.

Turning to the example of the GC, there the agenda is set by the women workers themselves and the projects that have been pursued have changed according to women's changing needs. While initially dealing just with issues of sexual harassment, Study A found numerous examples of where, to deal with the problem of low wages, the GCs had established rotating savings and credit associations (RoSCAs) to help workers save money and get interest-free loans from each other to pay for large expenses such as school fees or to buy food items such as maize in bulk. In two notable examples, one GC had set up a beekeeping project and a cooperatively run crèche, while another had set up a hotel that employed the children of workers who had finished school but were unable to find work.

What these examples show is that when women were given voice and power to influence the agenda, the kinds of projects that resulted were ones that were of benefit to the community as a whole. While this may not apply in all cases, it was found to be so in the case of workers in these Fairtrade certified tea and flower plantations in Kenya, highlighting the importance of ensuring a space for women within the JB.

Training and education

Training and education are crucial for empowerment as they help to build the capacities of women to act both in their own best interests and in those of their fellow women. Other than the purchasing of things (from T-shirts to crèches), the Fairtrade premium has also been used to fund various courses for workers at certified farms. These have included IT training, establishing a kitchen garden, nutrition, and driving lessons. For these women courses were significant: 'You know this job is not forever,' said one woman, 'they can come to you one day and say you are fired. But if we have received these courses, like hairdressing, I know that I can sit down and braid someone's hair and that will give me the 20 shillings I need to buy milk for my child'.

Where there are low levels of educational attainment, training plays a crucial role in fostering empowerment. Training can help workers gain greater levels of self-confidence and knowledge about their rights and health issues, as well as practical skills, all of which are crucial in facilitating empowerment. At the workplace, '*Gender wame neutralize wanaume* [the gender committee has neutralized the men]' said one worker. 'It helps defeat traditions and cultures. We too have the right to work here. The women have been *taught*, we have that freedom'.

A training manual highlights: 'Capacity building, one of the requirements repeatedly found in the Fairtrade standards, is all and above about empowerment' (FLO, 2007b: 10).

Training funded by the Fairtrade premium is not just limited to courses, but also member training on the purpose of the premium as well as numeracy and literacy explicitly geared towards improving their ability to carry out their roles. However, at the time of this study, many members had not yet received this training, with one stating: 'Maybe once we go for this training, is when we will be able to come back to the farm with new ideas and teach the others that projects do not just have to be sleeping materials'.

Furthermore, only a few workers at a time are able to benefit from training offered through JB premium expenditure and due to the nature of the project selection, these are often men. When we look at the capacity building offered to the JB members themselves, there are no mechanisms in place for this training to be disseminated among the broader workforce and the benefits remain with the few.

In contrast, training delivered via the GCs have two main differences. The first is that the training offered to members is not just explicitly that which will help them to fulfil their roles as JB members, but also gives them a wider variety of skills that can help them both in the workplace and at home. Secondly, the GCs also act as a peer education tool, with management using committee members to disseminate training and information to the workforce at large. At meetings, GC members are taught by the company or by NGOs about a wide variety of issues including problem solving, conflict resolution, starting a business, budgeting, and health. After the meetings, they talk to their co-workers in their places of work (e.g. gender committee members from the greenhouses talk to greenhouse workers, etc.) and teach them what they have learned, thereby sharing knowledge with each other. While no time has been set aside for GC members to act as peer educators, they carry out these duties alongside their paid ones. Despite this, they were found to have been very effective in disseminating the education given to them, with women workers citing many examples (e.g. many women workers in flowers farms in Naivasha referred to training they had been given on how to start their own business).

There are, however, limitations within the GC model in terms of training. As the information dissemination occurs on a very informal, laissez-faire basis, the greater the proximity of women to each other and the lower the ratio of GC members to workers, the faster the transfusion of ideas between workers, and the easier the job becomes. This was especially evident within the tea plantations where one woman could represent hundreds of employees who worked over a large area, rarely in close proximity with each other. There, knowledge of the responsibilities and roles of the GC was low, penetration of the training was limited, and a handful of interviewees did not even know about the GC, showing the importance of adequate representation.

Training provided to GC members also contributes to empowerment by exposing them to new ideas and possibilities with respect to action that they can then use to improve both their own lives and those of their fellow workers. In contrast, the responsibilities of the JB members did not include passing their training on to the non-members and, as a result, the JBs were seen as being more closed by non-members.

The training given to the GC members, specifically targeted at issues that women face both in the workplace at home, has contributed significantly to women's power. Workplace training given to them has raised awareness about issues (such as HIV/Aids or sexual harassment) which impact worker health and well-being, while 'gender' targeted education has provided women with tools to overcome barriers caused by societal norms (e.g. training on how to start a business or be a good leader that is provided to GC members). As a result, the GC has managed to effect broader changes in gendered dynamics between male and female workers than the JB.

The peer educator model used by the GCs (whereby the benefits of training trickle down to non-members), as well as the nature of the training offered to members (that is both practical and gender aware) could also be applied within the context of JBs and would help them to empower a greater proportion of workers than the few who directly benefit from the training or items purchased with the premium funds.

Synthesis

FLO has recognized that Fairtrade standards mechanisms for hired labour need to interact more positively with social protection measures, including labour legislation, within the supplier countries. Greater dialogue with trade unions to avoid undermining collective bargaining is highlighted as part of the new strategy for hired labour, agreed in early 2012, as well as more flexibility in the use of the premium to reflect local conditions, e.g. to support living wages (FLO, 2012: 26). However, our analysis suggests that there is a need for Fairtrade to acknowledge the local context, including gender relations, and learn from good practice at the local level.

First, there is a need to enhance representation of women. The limited voice accorded to women workers in the JB hampers its efficacy in providing projects that are equally beneficial for men and women. Given the patriarchal nature of Kenyan society, it is important to acknowledge the gender dynamics within the JB and to take measures to build capacities of women workers so that they too can participate fully in the JB. Training should be given to all workers, once elected, to help challenge the prevailing negative view of women in leadership positions. Second, there is a need to ensure that training covers a wider range of topics and is more gender-aware and widespread. The training offered to JB members and general workers through short courses only benefits a small proportion of the workforce. More diverse training should be given to JB members that better equips them to deal with issues both inside and outside the workplace. Further, measures should be put in place to equip JB members to act as peer educators and disseminate their learning more widely so that the benefits do not accrue only to the few, though there may be challenges here given the limited literacy of some workers.

The third key area for action is wider dissemination of principles of Fairtrade and the original intentions for the premium. While we note that FLO recognizes the need for greater flexibility in premium expenditure, and also that the lack of a living wage means that proposed projects often focus on immediate needs, nevertheless, there was considerable evidence that workers did not understand the purposes of Fairtrade. This contributed to workers proposing short-term, individualistic projects. Representatives of FLO say that they have provided training to workers, but we argue that there is a need to re-evaluate the methods used in order to widen the impact of this training.

Membership of the JB could be a very empowering process for workers. Aside from the member training, JBs can contribute to enhanced women's power through increasing their ability to perceive themselves as agents of change, as well as by increasing members' self-confidence and making them strong role models for their fellow workers. The training and experience accrued by GC members (e.g. providing advice and counselling or mediation between injured parties) are useful both in the workplace and in their households and communities, where they are better able to deal with and resolve conflicts. Through these processes, membership of groups such as the GC and JB can be seen to contribute to women's empowerment.

Our analysis shows that the practice of standards differs from the plans and expectations of standards developers and that it is important to recognize that 'the process of interpreting requirements and adapting them to local conditions is far from straightforward, and this may well have consequences in terms of time and resources invested' (Aasprong et al., 2013: 94). The outcomes of standards are influenced by 'horizontal governance' processes, such as means of monitoring or promoting compliance, as much as the designs of the standard setters (Tallontire et al., 2011). In the cases examined here, some of the choices by the JB were reinforcing gender divisions and offered limited opportunities to build up collective action by workers.

Conclusion

There is potential for standards mechanisms to inform each other; a form of positive 'entanglement' (Aasprong et al., 2013) between standards that draws on local best practice. Our analysis has unpacked how two standards mechanisms empower women workers and through this has highlighted some ways in which the JB can learn from the empowering processes identified in the GC.

An irony of our study is that a mechanism developed to assist social auditing and that was initiated in a top-down manner by company management has demonstrated greater empowerment pathways than a standards mechanism that is explicitly designed to empower workers, especially if gender is considered.

Given the embedded gender inequalities in Kenyan society, it is important that Fairtrade recognizes this and develops means to counteract it in standards mechanisms such as the JB. Our analysis suggests it is important for Fairtrade practices to recognize and engage with local norms and practices, particularly unequal gender relations, so that the benefits of Fairtrade can be enhanced, and to limit the potential for these benefits to be undermined.

The main implication of this analysis for standards bodies, in terms of enhancing the empowering effects of standards mechanisms, is that they need to ensure that all relevant workers are able to shape, benefit from, and participate in the JBs, actively building up the capacity of workers to engage so that they can be part of a process of self-empowerment. Training of committee members so that they are better able to represent all constituencies of workers is central to this.

About the authors

Muhaimina Said-Allsopp is a Research Fellow at Leeds University Business School where she works on green supply chains. Her PhD analysed women worker empowerment within the Kenyan tea and floriculture industries.

Anne Tallontire is a Senior Lecturer in Business, Environment and Corporate Social Responsibility at the School of Earth and Environment at Leeds University. She has worked on fair trade and standards for over 15 years.

References

Aasprong, H., Bain, C., Ransom, E. and Higgins, V. (2013) 'Entangled standardizing networks: the case of GLOBALGAP and fairtrade in St Vincent's banana industry', *International Journal of Sociology of Agriculture and Food* 20: 91–108 <www.ijsaf.org/archive/20/1/aasprong.pdf>.

Center for Evaluation (2012) *Assessing the Impact of Fairtrade on Poverty Reduction through Rural Development*, Final Report, Fairtrade Impact Study, Koln: TransFair Germany; Basel, Switzerland: Max Havelaar Foundation.

Fisher, E., Sheppard, H., Bain, C., Ransom, E. and Higgins, V. (2013) 'Pushing the boundaries of the social: private agri-food standards and the governance of fair trade in European public procurement', *International Journal of Sociology of Agriculture and Food* 20: 31–49 <www.ijsaf.org/archive/20/1/fisher_sheppard.pdf>.

Fairtrade International (FLO) (2007a) *Explanatory Document for the Fairtrade Premium and Joint Body in Hired Labour Situations*, Bonn, Germany: Fairtrade International.

FLO (2007b) *FLO Training Manual 2.0: Introduction into the Generic Fairtrade Standards for Hired Labour* (without environmental part), Bonn, Germany: Fairtrade International.

FLO (2010) *Consultation Document for Fairtrade Stakeholders: New Standards Framework*, Bonn, Germany: Fairtrade International.

FLO (2012) *Monitoring the Scope and Benefits of Fairtrade*, 4th edn, Bonn, Germany: Fairtrade International.

KHRC (2012) *'Wilting in Bloom'; The Irony of Women Labour Rights in the Cut-flower Sector in Kenya*, Nairobi: Kenya Human Rights Commission.

Loconto, A. (2010) 'Sustainably performed: reconciling global value chain governance and performativity', *Journal of Rural Social Sciences* 25: 193–225 <www.ag.auburn.edu/auxiliary/srsa/pages/Chapters/JRSS%202010%20 25%203%20193-225.pdf>.

Nelson, V. and Martin, A. (2012) 'The impact of Fairtrade: evidence, shaping factors, and future pathways', *Food Chain* 2: 42–63 <http://dx.doi.org/10.3362/2046-1887.2012.005>.

Nelson, V. and Pound, B. (2009) *The Last Ten Years: A Comprehensive Review of the Literature on the Impact of Fairtrade*, Chatham, UK: Natural Resources Institute, University of Greenwich.

Ochieng, B.O., Hughey, K.F.D. and Bigsby, H. (2013) 'Rainforest Alliance Certification of Kenyan tea farms: a contribution to sustainability or tokenism?' *Journal of Cleaner Production* 39: 285–93 <http://dx.doi.org/10.1016/j.jclepro.2012.07.048>.

Ouma, S. (2010) 'Global standards, local realities: private agrifood governance and the restructuring of the Kenyan horticulture industry', *Economic Geography* 86: 197–222 <http://dx.doi.org/10.1111/j.1944-8287.2009.01065.x>.

Riisgaard, L. (2009) 'Global value chains, labor organization and private social standards: lessons from East African cut flower industries', *World Development* 37: 326–40 <http://dx.doi.org/10.1016/j.worlddev.2008.03.003>.

Riisgaard, L. (2011) 'Towards more stringent sustainability standards? Trends in the cut flower industry', *Review of African Political Economy* 38: 435–53 <http://dx.doi.org/10.1080/03056244.2011.598344>.

Said-Allsopp, M. (2013) *Empowerment within Global Value Chains: A Study of the Dynamics of Employment and its Impacts on the Lives of Women Employed in Kenyan Agricultural Export Industries*, PhD thesis: School of Earth and Environment, University of Leeds.

Tallontire, A. and Said-Allsopp, M. (2013) *Global Value Chains and Empowerment Value Chains: Insights from Women Workers in Kenyan Floriculture*. Presented at the 2nd workshop on Integrating Labour and Skills into Global Value Chains, Centre for Research on the Economy of the Workplace, University of Birmingham.

Tallontire, A., Dolan, C., Smith, S. and Barrientos, S. (2005) 'Reaching the marginalised? Gender value chains and ethical trade in African horticulture', *Development in Practice* 15: 559–71 <http://dx.doi.org/10.1080/09614520500075771>.

Tallontire, A., Opondo, M., Nelson, V. and Martin, A. (2011) 'Beyond the vertical? Using value chains and governance as a framework to analyse private standards initiatives in agri-food chains', *Agriculture and Human Values* 28: 427–41 <http://dx.doi.org/10.1007/s10460-009-9237-2>.

CHAPTER 6

Access to the Fairtrade system: the geography of certification for social justice

Alastair M. Smith

Abstract

A growing body of research and analysis identifies that fair trade practices create opportunities for developing world producers in a manner best described as providing 'shaped advantage', as access to Northern markets is reconfigured to operate under preferable conditions for some producers, but is not necessarily universally expanded and improved. From this point of view, impact potential is first and foremost delineated through the conditions of access to fair trade supply networks. In order to unpack this perspective, the chapter analyses barriers to entry embedded in the most significant avenue through which producers become involved in fair trade: certification by Fairtrade International. Here it is found that in addition to arguably justifiable restrictions on participation, structured around producer capacity to viably engage in trade, more arbitrary geographical restrictions embedded in the Fairtrade system are also an ongoing and significant barrier to widening impact. This chapter illustrates the reality of these technical limitations by presenting the mixed experiences of the National Smallholder Farmers' Association of Malawi, and their efforts to use Fairtrade certification as a market development tool.

Keywords: fair trade, Fairtrade International, certification, market access, impact

THERE IS GROWING RECOGNITION that in their current form, fair trade practices offer a form of 'shaped advantage' by which a limited number of developing world producers engage with global markets under more favourable terms. More specifically, the fair trade system is understood to support these producers in 'utilizing enhanced institutional capacity and marketing skills to tap into a growing niche market' (Lyon and Moberg 2010: 8). Based on this perspective, one of the most fundamental factors governing the impact of fair trade is the ability of individual producers, and their wider groupings, to participate in supply chains operating on the basis of associated principles. Where this issue of access has been considered, there is concern that the capacity of producers might be a key variable in their ability to benefit, and that therefore,

http://dx.doi.org/10.3362/9781780449067.006

'geographic marginality may work against successful participation' (Nelson and Martin 2012: 47). In an effort to specifically address these issues, this chapter provides an in-depth analysis of the factors governing producer access to Fairtrade International certification and, therefore, the primary means through which participation in fair trade is likely to occur. Although a number of key factors are considered, the chapter focuses on geographical limitations to the availability of certification, and illustrates this through a case study of the National Smallholder Farmers' Association of Malawi.

Fairtrade certification: the falling barriers to participation

Fair trade began as European and North American organizations, dedicated to improving levels of welfare in the developing world, began to see the purchase of handicraft and food goods from target communities as a tool to practise their wider mission. In contrast to conventional commercial operations, which aimed to maximize the gain of the buyer, these trade practices were specifically structured around conditions believed to be beneficial for producers. At this time, fair, or alternative trade as it was then often referred to, was confined to supply chains operated by socially orientated organizations. On this basis, impact was highly restricted: both to areas of the developing world where such organizations had existing networks, and by the limited market into which such organizations sold their goods. Seeking to overcome these limitations, a partnership between Solidaridad (a Dutch NGO) and a community of Mexican coffee farmers developed a system of third party certification for fair trade coffee (Fridell, 2007: 186–87). First appearing as the *Max Havelaar* Mark, this approach was an innovation as by focusing on the condition of initial purchase, fair trade goods could be commercialized through supply chains under mainstream commercial governance arrangements, including final sale by retailers providing for mass consumer markets (Smith, 2013a). Given the success of this model, it was subsequently reproduced in other European and North American 'consumer' countries (plus Japan). Later, the separate mechanisms of these national initiatives were centralized under the Fairtrade Labelling Organizations International (FLO), which is today known as Fairtrade International (Renard, 2005: 425).

While the requirements of Fairtrade certification are now highly complex, in summary, the system governs certain aspects of the trade relationship between Southern producer organizations and Northern importers. Of importance to the analysis below, Fairtrade requires the payment of a Social Premium in addition to the basic price to fund development investments by the producer organization; in some cases the system also sets minimum prices per unit of goods sold and requires the provision of upfront credit by the buyer (Doherty et al., 2012: 4). For an overview of how an individual product might be certified see Smith (2011: 46–7).

Initially, certification only applied to coffee and was still restricted to collective cooperative organizations of small producers already connected to alternative trade networks. In the UK certification was also focused on supply chains coordinated by small and medium intermediary organizations with a particular interest in promoting welfare in the developing world (Davies, 2007: 465). However, as the certification system grew, the range of products covered has expanded, and in 2012 standards existed for over 300 raw products (Fairtrade International, 2012: 8). Likewise, pushing to expand impact through growing volumes, the Fairtrade system has aimed to involve more commercial operations higher in the supply chain, and companies that now carry the Fairtrade mark on some of their product lines include: Starbucks, Nestlé, Dole, Cadbury and Fyffes (Meyer, 2013). Given that these companies required larger volumes of products with more consistent quality standards, certification was also extended to products from plantations and other hired labour situations. In addition, in order to account for goods produced with a combination of family and hired labour (Luetchford, 2008), the definition of Small Producers was further revised in 2009 to allow for this (Smith, 2010). For a combination of these reasons, by 2012 Fairtrade International certified products sourced from some 991 producer organizations, and in turn around 1.2 million farmers and workers in the developing world (Fairtrade International, 2012: 3). As a result, in 2012 the retail sales of Fairtrade certified goods generated around €5.5 bn across over 120 countries and 6,000 product lines (Fairtrade International, 2012: 3; Meyer, 2013).

Although the above changes and current mechanisms have greatly expanded producer access to Fairtrade certification, hundreds of thousands of producers in the developing world are still excluded on the basis of their current livelihood capacities (Davenport and Low, 2012: 11). Furthermore, new issues that limit participation by producers have developed. With the increasing involvement of commercial organizations higher in the supply chain, greater emphasis has been placed on the retrospective certification of organizations that already have the capacity to supply goods to mainstream commercial standards (Fairtrade International, 2011b, c); moreover, this requirement is considered to exclude many of the poorest individual producers and their organizations. Although there is some case study evidence that groups with very limited levels of capacity can obtain and benefit from Fairtrade certification (Imhof and Lee, 2007; Ronchi, 2002), senior representatives of Fairtrade International note that 'one of the challenges that we face is that there are a lot of producers around who don't fit into the current model'. Indeed, interviews with senior officials identify that the need to open up access is understood as a fundamental issue of credibility for the organization.

In recognition of the need to make the certification system more accessible, Fairtrade International introduced the Contract Standard. This specific certification is available for producer groups that initially lack the capacity to comply with standard Fairtrade requirements, perhaps because they are not democratically organized. The standard allows such groups to sell Fairtrade certified goods if they meet a reduced set of requirements while working in partnership with a support organization, such as an export organization or an NGO, to build the necessary capacities for full certification (Fairtrade International, 2011a).

Another change in the system that affected conditions of access to certification came between 2004 and 2006 when, following the impetus to expand the volumes of Fairtrade certified goods, there was a shift away from the complete subsidization of producer certification fees by buyers (Hutchens, 2009: 66). As a result, in 2007 applications by producer groups required an upfront payment of €250 and cost around €350 per day for certification audits (Neilson and Pritchard, 2010: 1848). By 2011, coordination and evaluation of an initial application had reached the current (2013) cost of €525 – which covers the administration of the initial application and is therefore not refunded if application is rejected, although is only chargeable once irrespective of the number of products or commercial functions for which an organization applies (FLO-CERT, 2011: 5). While certification fees now vary significantly by type and size of organization (FLO-CERT, 2013a, b, c), a breakdown of the basic certification costs can be seen in Table 6.1. Moreover, in 2013 the CEO of FLO-CERT (the organization responsible for inspecting and certifying producer organizations against the standards set by Fairtrade International) estimated the typical cost of Fairtrade certification for a producer group to be €2,520, or €1.44 per farmer/worker (Meyer, 2013). However, those wishing to operate as a trader of Fairtrade certified goods are charged a slightly higher fee of €2,735 as a means to provide a small subsidy for producers on the true costs (Meyer, 2013). In order to further assist producer organizations with certification, Fairtrade International operates a Producer Certification Fund which provides a subsidy of up to 75 per cent for 'first order cooperatives' (those formed by the immediate producers of a good) seeking to be become certified for the first time (Fairtrade International, 2011e). In 2012, 131 cooperatives, including in Ghana and Mauritius, received a total of US$1 m to finance their certification (Fairtrade Africa, 2013). Despite these support mechanisms, however, many criticize the need for poor producers to pay towards the cost of a mechanism that is, in principle, provided for their support and development.

Table 6.1 Basic Fairtrade certification costs for small producer organizations

Number of members	Initial certification fee (€)	Subsequent annual certification fee (€)
<50	1,430	1,170
50–100	2,040	1,610
101–250	2,250	1,790
251–500	2,450	1,970
501–1000	3,060	2,410
> 1000	3,470	2,770

Source: FLO-CERT, 2013c

Geographical restrictions on Fairtrade certification

Despite expansion of the availability of Fairtrade certification, the focus of the Fairtrade system on specific products implies the differentiation of access on geographical terms, and this fundamentally limits the potential impact of the system. To begin with, Fairtrade International specifically highlights that 'Fairtrade Standards are limited to certain countries. [So]…only producers in these countries can apply for Fairtrade Certification' (Fairtrade International, 2011d). However, given the aim to alleviate poverty in the developing world through trade, 'Fairtrade International defines the countries in which it certifies producers as those countries with low and medium development status' based on the list provided by the OECD Development Assistance Committee (Fairtrade International, 2011g: 2). In this case, the broad geographical focus of Fairtrade is based on the perceived need of producers in economically less developed countries, and can therefore be understood as legitimate based on the analysis of 'need' and therefore, social justice. This is significant as other certification systems, such as Fair for Life, are not limited to the developing world and are also available to producers from high income countries (Smith, 2013c).

Within the focus on the developing world, however, there are further geographically defined limitations to the engagement of producers who could arguably benefit from involvement in the system. At the sub-national level in South India, for example, Neilson and Pritchard (2010: 1844) identified geographical limitations to the availability of Fairtrade certification in that, 'Tea estates abandoned and therefore not producing any tea fell outside the gaze of the fair and ethical trade movement' (Neilson and Pritchard, 2010: 1849). Therefore, it is argued that those individuals in the developing world arguably most in need, are not considered by Fairtrade at all. While this point is self-reflexively identified as a harsh evaluation by the authors, it is an important issue for consideration by Northern consumers. The focus on the Southern poor working in livelihoods that produce for wealthy markets certainly violates a needs-based approach to targeting interventions and, for this reason, it is important that participation in ethical consumption does not undermine wider, more encompassing interventions. On a more pertinent level of evaluation, however, there are a number of empirical investigations that have highlighted that access to fair trade markets through the Fairtrade system is often dictated by market and retailer demands rather than producer need (Fridell, 2004: 153). This is found to be the case in supply chains where products are ultimately retailed by supermarkets that have a very specific way in which they wish to construct the brands of their products. For example, when UK supermarket Tesco began buying bananas from the Windward Islands, they overrode the producer organization's internal decision to allocate export quotas equally across islands, instead insisting on sourcing the majority of fruit from Dominica, as this fitted with their branding requirements (Moberg, 2005: 10).

The question of opportunity to obtain Fairtrade certification is important given the primary aim of the movement to develop market access for those developing world producers otherwise less able to benefit from international supply networks. Although the Fairtrade system does not expressly aim to work with those producers that are most in need, the question to what extent this is required for the approach to carry legitimacy has been highlighted by commentators. In the past Fairtrade International was criticized for not having certification available to lower income countries such as Ethiopia, but instead certifying the majority of goods in relatively more wealthy parts of the world such as Mexico (Sidwell, 2008: 11). Although the relevance of this argument has been well countered from a number of angles (Smith, 2009: 30), Fairtrade International has continued to make investments to expand the geographic scope of its operation (see discussion in Smith, 2008: 23). Five years on in 2013, Fairtrade International certification is available in over 70 countries. Furthermore, analysis of the United Nations current list of Least Developed Countries (LDCs) shows that all these, apart from South Sudan (which only became an independent state in July 2011), now have some Fairtrade International product certification available to them (Compare: Fairtrade International, 2011g; UN-OHRLLS, 2013).

Despite the widening of Fairtrade's scope, which now includes even small producer organizations (SPOs) in China (Fairtrade International, 2011g: 2), this does not mean that non-needs-based geographical limitations have been entirely removed. For example, although the Producer Certification Fund (see above) provides priority for groups from the Least Developed Countries (LDC) (Fairtrade International, 2011f: 2), there are also additional priorities for the support of certain product types from specific geographical locations (these are outlined in Table 6.2).

More significantly, however, not all Fairtrade International standards are available in every developing world country, and this is also true for those that are the least developed. Although some product standards are available throughout the developing world, the majority remain restricted by geographical location; a summary of the majority of these, although not all, is provided in Appendix 1.

In some cases, certain products can only be certified for production in certain countries. For example, grapefruit is only certifiable by producers in Mexico, South Africa, and Northern Africa. Although in this situation produce can be

Table 6.2 Geographical and product priorities for certification support

Product	Geographical specification
Bananas, organic juices, orange juice, sugar, cotton	All countries
Cocoa	Ecuador, México, Venezuela, Haití, Dom. Republic, Nicaragua, Africa
Vanilla	Madagascar, Indonesia, Papua New Guinea
Dried fruit	West Africa

Source: Fairtrade International, 2011f: 2–3

organic or sourced from SPOs and hired labour (HL) organizations, in other cases the availability of certification is differentiated by both geography and product characteristics. For example, while only organic raisins from SPOs can be certi-fied in South Africa, SPOs in Southern Asia, Central Asia and South America can also obtain endorsements for conventional raisins. Finally, in some cases, such as pineapple for drying, although organic and conventional produce in Eastern Africa, Middle Africa, South America, South-eastern Asia, Southern Asia, the Caribbean, and most of Western Africa must be from SPOs, HL production in Ghana is also certifiable. In some situations, the unavailability of certification might reflect the lack of production in a particular country. However, in other cases, the lack of opportunity to apply for certification is due to other admin-istrative issues and, in most cases, the need to establish the details of standards that are specific to the country, and is therefore most likely the result of the Fairtrade International system having no established Fairtrade price or Social Premium for the local context. Where this occurs, however, in principle there is the option for stakeholders to apply for the geographical extension of standards to new countries through one of three possible administrative procedures:

- *Full price research.* The standard procedure which includes a Costs of Sus-tainable Production analysis and can be used in all cases and for all types of products.
- *Easy entrance.* Applied for new products in existing standards, such as: 1) when the product description, trade characteristics and producer set-up fit into the scope of existing standards; 2) minor products; 3) where risks to using this method are low.
- *Price extension.* Used to fill pricing gaps in existing Fairtrade product standards including between different geographical locations and for calculating organic differentials (see: Fairtrade International, 2011h).

In summary, the above section highlights the ways in which access to Fairtrade certification is restricted by capacity, but also geography and product charac-teristics; although it is noted that in the case of geographical limitations there are options for flexibility in the current arrangements. In order to illustrate how this situation is played out in producer realities, however, the following section provides a case study of the experience of the National Smallholder Farmers' Association in Malawi. Here it is highlighted that more needs to be done by Fairtrade International to develop a needs-based approach to certifi-cation availability.

Case study: The National Smallholder Farmers' Association of Malawi (NASFAM)

Malawi is a landlocked country in southern Africa, currently classified by the United Nations as one of the poorest and Least Developed Countries in the world. In 2012, the Human Development Report ranked the country 170 out of 186 (UNDP, 2012a) – having moved up one place since the previous assessment. The gross national product per capita of Malawi is currently $774, with 73.9 per cent of the population living below the $1.25 per day poverty line (UNDP, 2012b). In 2011, growth in real gross domestic product (GDP) slowed to 4.3 per cent from 6.3 per cent in 2010 on account of foreign exchange and fuel shortages, issues symptomatic of Malawi's structural reliance on agricultural exports (suffering from volatile and declining real prices) and imported mineral fuels (African Economic Outlook, 2013). Very little of the country's population lives in urban areas (15.8 per cent), and overall, agriculture accounts for a significant part of economic activity, 70 per cent of which is undertaken by smallholder producers. Although there is emerging evidence that this model is not in itself fundamentally restrictive of economic performance in sub-Saharan Africa (Moyo and Chambati, 2013), Malawian smallholder farmers have been subjected to decades of marginalization (Smith, 2013b: 118–9). From the absorption of present day Malawi into the British Empire, smallholder farmers have been continually hampered by legal restrictions on their activities, and independence in 1964 is only considered to have extended the exploitation of smallholders (Kydd and Christiansen, 1982). Despite reforms of inefficient state-administered agricultural support and marketing mechanisms in the 1980s, it is widely considered that productivity was not enhanced given a lack of capacity in the private sector (Devereux and Tiba, 2007: 165; Kutengule et al., 2013: 421). Where traders did emerge, they were reportedly mostly unlicensed vendors benefiting from information asymmetries and fixed weights and measures, therefore largely exacerbating a long history of exploitative intermediaries in the agricultural marketing sector (See: McCracken, 1983: 178).

Following the liberalization programme, the United States Agency for International Development (USAID) funded a 'Smallholder Agribusiness Development Project' (SADP) in 1995. The intention was to strengthen smallholder capacity to take advantage of opportunities provided by liberalization, and the success of the programme resulted in the development of a permanent support organization in 1998: the National Smallholder Farmers' Association of Malawi (NASFAM) (Smith, 2013b: 119). Overall NASFAM is a financial trust owned by its approximately 100,000 farmer members, who are organized into local associations, in turn comprising village level clubs containing around 10 to 20 individuals. NASFAM functions practically through two subsidiaries, one of which focuses on capacity building, and the other on the supply of seed and the marketing of members' crops. Given the democratic organization of the overall entity, NASFAM's commercial arm offers a guaranteed market for members' produce at the end of the season and bases prices derived from cost of production analysis (Smith, 2011).

Given the historical reliance of individual farmers, and the country as a whole, on a narrow range of agricultural crops (primarily tobacco), one of NASFAM's primary aims is to facilitate diversification (Smith, 2013b). Speaking about the issues at the macro level during an interview, NASFAM's Commercial Manager summarizes that:

> We need to move away from the traditional exports, tobacco 500, 600 million dollars, that is more than half of the FOREX, I think, and a sane country should be running away from that situation. We can still maintain it at 600 million but that shouldn't be 50 percent of our exports. We need to look at how we can create a 300 million export market, a 200 million, a 100 million et cetera.

Another agricultural commodity traditionally exported by Malawi is groundnuts, or peanuts, as they are sometimes known. However, alongside increasing international competition, Malawian production was cut out of Europe following the discovery of a widespread aflatoxin infection in the mid-1990s. This is a by-product of a ubiquitous fungus which grows on a wide range of Southern commodity foods, and is encouraged by poor husbandry, particularly for example, when producers moisten nuts to facilitate shelling. However, due to its carcinogenic nature, detection of aflatoxin understandably prompted stringent regulation from the traditional import markets in Europe. Unable to deal with the problem without support, Malawian exports to the continent crashed entirely until NASFAM identified fair trade practices as one possible means to restore this previously lucrative export sector.

More specifically, partnering with a mission-driven fair trade organization (TWIN Trading, based in London, UK), NASFAM worked to certify the Mchinji Area Smallholder Farmers' Association (MASFA) as a producers cooperative, and the commercial company as a registered exporter. Through this relationship, NASFAM benefited from support to address the aflatoxin risks and also developed new trade relationships with major UK supermarkets (Smith, 2013b: 120–21).

Despite this particular success, however, the limitations on access to Fairtrade certification began to become apparent to NASFAM as they developed an interest in extending involvement to other associations. To begin with, although the investment in Fairtrade certification for MASFA showed good returns in the long term, the cost of this process was not easily shouldered. Moreover, interest in certifying a second association at Mzimba stalled due to a lack of funds to cover the costs of certification. In reference to this case, a senior manager explained during an interview that 'we have an association, a very productive association – we just don't have on any of the budgets around 3,000 Euros to certify them. We have already paid a bit for the audit, [although] if we don't certify this year, we'll have to start [again] from scratch'.

Given the imperative to diversify exports, NASFAM's management also identified advantages in obtaining fair trade markets for another of its core products: Kilombero rice. A long-grain variety of brown rice, Kilombero is eaten alongside maize as a staple food in northern Malawi, although, given its versatile and aromatic nature, the product was considered an excellent candidate to become a high value export for Europe (Smith, 2011: 125 & 143). Although funding was an issue, it was also understood by management that certification would be impossible. This was because, as can be seen from Appendix 1, only producer groups located in Thailand, Laos, India, and Egypt can readily apply for certification for certain varieties of rice. Therefore, before certification could be applied for, it was necessary to arrange for the product standard to be extended to Malawi (using one of the procedures outlined above). However, despite approaches made to the regional Fairtrade Liaison Officer to initiate the extension process, no mention of these possibilities was made. Moreover, the request was met with the response that nothing could be done until the next Fairtrade International price review meeting, although no preparatory measures were ever suggested. In this case, it was the view of a number of direct stakeholders, and unconnected informants working in the area more generally, that Fairtrade capacity to support producers with such issues in this region was currently lacking. An alternative interpretation, however, is that although exports were already under way to Scotland in the UK, the costs involved in geographical extension were not viewed by Fairtrade decision-makers as an appropriate investment (Smith, 2013a).

Irrespective of the cause of the lack of engagement by Fairtrade International, there is concern among stakeholders in the incipient supply chain that despite efforts to develop physical capacity for export, the work to create the market in the UK is placed at a disadvantage without the ability to obtain Fairtrade certification. During interviews, stakeholders identified their efforts as working very much in line with the principles of the fair trade system. One interviewee working with a partner NGO to NASFAM noted that the rice 'is from smallholder farmers through a reputable smallholder organization so the general framework is there', which as mentioned above, includes that producers are members of a democratically organized organization through which they negotiate yearly prices based on the costs of production. Furthermore, the UK-based importer of the Kilombero rice pays NASFAM Commercial an export price which reflects the internal price setting dynamics, and also covers the export costs. Indeed, at the time of research, the importer had made it a point of principle not to negotiate on the price requested, and this resulted in a price in excess of the minimums stipulated under Fairtrade standards for other countries. Despite these practices, however, there was concern among stakeholders that without Fairtrade certification to recognize them, end consumers and intermediary retailers may not understand the ethical credentials of the product. This is because stakeholders, including a representative of TWIN Trading, recognize that 'the challenge with all of these things when you are talking about consumer branding, is...[that] people only have so much head space'. For this reason, although there is acceptance that great progress has been made selling to consumers particularly attuned with the broader fair trade message – such as those with a long association with fair trade or networked through church groups, etc. – it would be much harder to successfully engage with more mainstream markets. Indeed, action research highlights that even those members of the fair trade movement with more significant knowledge are often reluctant to break away from their reliance on the Fairtrade mark in understanding what constitutes a legitimate fair trade product. It is for this reason that stakeholders working with NASFAM to build the Kilombero rice supply chain feel that '[this] is where the major market is', and therefore that Fairtrade International certification would be of great significance to expand the impact of their work.

Conclusion

There is an emerging view that fair trade offers 'shaped advantage' to a limited selection of developing world producers who benefit from improved levels of market access and supply chain conditions. In many ways, the potential for impact within these arrangements has grown significantly as the fair trade movement has developed from a very small collection of closed trade circuits, to gradually penetrate conventionally operated systems of commercialization. This has been largely facilitated by the development of the third party certification system now administered by Fairtrade International. Although the initial geographical and product scope of this system was significantly limited, this has expanded considerably to the stage where over 300 product categories are available across the developing world. Within this development, however, this chapter has identified variables that continue to limit the potential for producer involvement. Some of these are located in the characteristics of producer communities themselves – and range from the broad nature of livelihood activities to the capacity with which these are carried out. Beyond basic eligibility, significant factors limiting access to Fairtrade certification are the ability of producers to meet the required quality standards and also afford the new costs of certification (which have been introduced as a perceived imperative for overall expansion of the system). However, in addition to these, this chapter has highlighted that at the current time, many of the Fairtrade standards are not immediately applicable to all geographical regions, either in their entirety or under certain physical and social conditions of production (being restricted to organic/conventional production, or supply by hired labour/small producer organizations in certain countries).

To some extent, these limitations on impact potential are recognized by Fairtrade International, which has therefore developed supportive mechanisms designed to refine the opportunities for access. For example, the introduction of a Contract Standard aims to help producer organizations lacking capacity to comply with the full requirements immediately, and the Producer Certification Fund subsidizes those unable to meet the financial costs involved. Beyond the existence of these mechanisms, however, it is not clear to what extent they reduce the barriers to entry. Indeed, although the documentation of the Fairtrade system highlights three means by which product standards can be geographically extended, the case study of NASFAM indicates that there is likely to be a gap between discourse and lived producer experience. This is a significant issue, as, given the growing demand for goods specifically certified by Fairtrade International in core consumer countries, producers unable to access certification feel greatly disadvantaged.

As a result of the above analysis, it is suggested that more work be done to understand the degree to which poor producers are isolated from participation in the Fairtrade system for reasons that run counter to a needs-based approach to certification availability. Where this is found to be the case, it will be important for Fairtrade International to continue to expand the geographical scope of its certification. Indeed, increasing levels of access will be an essential part of developing the Fairtrade system from a marketing and developmental niche, to an increasingly meaningful part of a wider movement for fairer international trade.

About the author

Alastair M. Smith is a Research Fellow at Cardiff School of Planning and Geography, Cardiff, UK.

References

African Economic Outlook (2013) *Malawi* [online] <www.africaneconomi-coutlook.org/en/countries/southern-africa/malawi/> [accessed 16 January 2014].

Davenport, E. and Low, W. (2012) 'The World Fair Trade Organization: from trust to compliance', in D. Reed, P. Utting and A. Mukherjee-Reed (eds), *Business Regulation, Non-State Actors and Development: Whose Standards? Whose Development?* London: Routledge.

Davies, I.A. (2007) 'The eras and participants of fair trade: an industry structure/stakeholder perspective on the growth of the fair trade industry', *Corporate Governance Journal* 7(4): 455–70 <http://dx.doi.org/10.1108/147 20700710820533>.

Devereux, S. and Tiba, Z. (2007) 'Malawi's first famine, 2001–2002', in S. Devereux (ed.), *The New Famines: Why Famines Persist in an Era of Globalization*, pp. 143–77, London and New York: Routledge.

Doherty, B., Davies, I.A. and Tranchell, S. (2012) 'Where now for fair trade?' *Business History* 55: 169–89 <http://dx.doi.org/10.1080/00076791.2012.69 2083>.

Fairtrade Africa (2013) *Did You Know about the Certification Fund?* [online] <www.fairtradeafrica.net/news/did-you-know-about-the-certification-fund/> [accessed 20 August 2013].

Fairtrade International (FLO) (2011a) *Fairtrade Standard for Contract Production*, Bonn, Germany: FLO.

FLO (2011b) *Fairtrade Standard for Hired Labour*, Bonn, Germany: FLO.

FLO (2011c) *Fairtrade Standard for Small Producer Organizations*, Bonn, Germany: FLO.

FLO (2011d) *Our standards* [online] <www.fairtrade.net/our-standards.html> [accessed 16 January 2014].

FLO (2011e) *Producer Certification Fund* [online] <www.fairtrade.net/producer-certification-fund.html> [accessed 12 August 2013].

FLO (2011f) *Guidelines: The Producer Certification Fund* [pdf] <www.fairtrade.net/fileadmin/user_upload/content/2009/producers/2011-PCF_Guidelines-EN.pdf> [accessed 16 January 2014].

FLO (2011g) *Geographical Scope of Producer Certification for Fairtrade Labelling*, Bonn, Germany: FLO.

FLO (2011h) *Standard Operating Procedure: Development of Fairtrade minimum prices and premiums* [pdf] <www.share4dev.info/kb/documents/5098.pdf> [accessed 16 January 2014].

FLO (2012) *For Producers, With Producers: Annual Report 2011–12* [pdf] Bonn, Germany: Fairtrade International <www.fairtrade.net/fileadmin/user_upload/content/2009/resources/2011-12_AnnualReport_web_version_small_FairtradeInternational.pdf> [accessed 16 January 2014].

Hutchens, A. (2009) *Changing Big Business: The Globalisation of the Fair Trade Movement*, Cheltenham: Edward Elgar Publishing.

FLO-CERT (2011) *Application for Fairtrade Certification Standard Operating Procedure* [pdf] <www.flo-cert.net/flo-cert/fileadmin/user_upload/certification/processes/application/CERT_Application_SOP_12_en.pdf> [accessed 16 January 2014].

FLO-CERT (2013a) *Fee System Contract Production: Explanatory Document* [pdf] <www.flo-cert.net/flo-cert/fileadmin/user_upload/certification/cost/en/PC_FeeSysCP_ED_17_en.pdf> [accessed 16 January 2014].

FLO-CERT (2013b) *Fee System Hired Labour: Explanatory Document* [pdf] <www.flo-cert.net/flo-cert/fileadmin/user_upload/certification/cost/en/PC_FeeSysHL_ED_25_en.pdf> [accessed 16 January 2014].

FLO-CERT (2013c) *Fee System Small Producer Organization Explanatory Document* [pdf] <www.flo-cert.net/flo-cert/fileadmin/user_upload/certification/cost/en/PC_FeeSysSPO_ED_24_en.pdf> [accessed 16 January 2014].

Fridell, G. (2004) 'The university and the moral imperative of fair trade coffee', *Journal of Academic Ethics* 2(1): 141–59 <http://dx.doi.org/10.1023/B:JAET.0000039012.55533.04>.

Fridell, G. (2007) *Fair Trade Coffee: The Prospects and Pitfalls of Market Driven Justice*, London: University of Toronto.

Imhof, S. and Lee, A. (2007) *Assessing the Potential of Fair Trade for Poverty Reduction and Conflict Prevention: A Case Study of Bolivian Coffee Producers* [online] Eldis <www.eldis.org/go/country-profiles&id=33539&type=Document#.Ugqib6wUuSo> [accessed 16 January 2014].

Kutengule, M., Nionucifora, A. and Zaman, H. (2013) 'Malawi: agricultural development and marketing corporation reform', in A. Coudouel, A.A. Dani and S. Paternostro (eds), *Poverty and Social Impact Analysis of Reforms: Lessons and Examples from Implementation*, pp. 415–52, Washington, DC: World Bank.

Kydd, J. and Christiansen, R. (1982) 'Structural change in Malawi since independence: consequences of a development strategy based on large-scale agriculture', *World Development* 10(5): 355–75 <http://dx.doi.org/10.1016/0305-750X(82)90083-3>.

Luetchford, P. (2008) 'The hands that pick fair trade coffee: beyond the charms of the family farm', in P. Luetchford and G.D. Neve (eds), *Hidden Hands in the Market: Ethnographies of Fair Trade, Ethical Consumption and Corporate Social Responsibility*, Vol. 28, pp. 143–69, Bingley: Emerald Publishing Group Limited.

Lyon, S. and Moberg, M. (eds) (2010) *Fair Trade and Social Justice: Global Ethnographies*, New York: New York University Press.

McCracken, J. (1983) 'Planters, peasants and the colonial state: the impact of the native tobacco board in the central province of Malawi', *Journal of Southern African Studies* 9(2): 172–92 <www.jstor.org/stable/2636299>.

Meyer, R. (ed.) (2013) 'FLO-CERT', *12th World Fair Trade Organization Biennial Conference,* Rio de Janeiro, Brazil.

Moberg, M. (2005) 'Fair trade and Eastern Caribbean banana farmers: rhetoric and reality in the anti-globalization movement', *Human Organization* 64(1): 4–15 <http://sfaa.metapress.com/content/j8ad5ffqqktq102g/>.

Moyo, S. and Chambati, W. (eds) (2013) *Land and Agrarian Reform in Zimbabwe: Beyond White Settler Capitalism,* Dakar: CODESRIA & AIAS.

Neilson, J. and Pritchard, B. (2010) 'Fairness and ethicality in their place: the regional dynamics of fair trade and ethical sourcing agendas in the plantation districts of South India', *Environment and Planning A* 42(8): 1833–51 <http://dx.doi.org/10.1068/a4260>.

Nelson, V. and Martin, A. (2012) The impact of fairtrade: evidence, shaping factors, and future pathways', *Food Chain* 2(1): 42–63 <http://dx.doi.org/10.3362/2046-1887.2012.005>.

Renard, M.-C. (2005) 'Quality certification, regulation and power in fair trade', *Journal of Rural Studies* 21(4): 419–31 <http://dx.doi.org/10.1016/j.jrurstud.2005.09.002>.

Ronchi, L. (2002) *The Impact of Fair Trade on Producers and Their Organizations: A Case Study with Coocafe in Costa Rica*, Brighton, UK: University of Sussex.

Sidwell, M. (2008) *Unfair Trade*, London: Adam Smith Institute.

Smith, A.M. (2008) *The Fair Trade Cup is 'Two-Thirds Full' not 'Two-Thirds Empty': A response to the Adam Smith Report & a new way to think about measuring the content of the Fair Trade Cup* [online] Comment and Analysis, ESRC Centre for Business Relationships, Accountability, Sustainability and Society, Cardiff University <http://orca.cf.ac.uk/49953/> [accessed 27 September 2010].

Smith, A.M. (2009) 'Evaluating the criticisms of fair trade: how strong is the argument that consumers and businesses should abandon fair trade as a means to socialise their economic decisions?' *Economic Affairs* 19(4): 62–4 <http://dx.doi.org/10.1111/j.1468-0270.2009.01944.x>.

Smith, A.M. (2010) *Responding to Commentary? Changes in the Regulations of the Fairtrade Labelling Organizations International (on defining small farmers and development practice)* [online], BRASS Comment and Analysis, Cardiff, UK: ESRC Centre for Business, Relationships, Accountability, Sustainability and Society <http://citeseerx.ist.psu.edu/viewdoc/download?doi=10.1.1.173.6943&rep=rep1&type=pdf> [accessed 26 June 2010].

Smith, A.M. (2011) *Fair Trade, Public Procurement and Sustainable Development: A Case Study of Malawian rice in Scotland* [online], PhD thesis, School of Planning and Geography & ESRC Centre for Business Relationships, Sustainability and Society, Cardiff University <http://orca.cf.ac.uk/10706/> [accessed 16 January 2014].

Smith, A.M. (2013a) 'Cross-border innovation in south-north fair trade supply chains: the opportunities and problems of integrating fair trade governance into northern public procurement', in D.V. Brust, J. Sarkis and J. Cordeiro (eds), *Collaboration for Sustainability and Innovation in the Global South: A role for South-driven Sustainability?* London: Springer.

Smith, A.M. (2013b) 'Fair trade governance and diversification: the experience of the National Smallholder Farmers' Association of Malawi', *GeoForum* 48: 114–25 <http://dx.doi.org/10.1016/j.geoforum.2013.04.020>.

Smith, A.M. (2013c) 'What does it mean to do fair trade? Ontology, praxis, and the 'Fair for Life' certification system', *Social Enterprise Journal* 9(1): 53–72 <http://dx.doi.org/10.1108/17508611311330000>.

United Nations Development Programme (UNDP) (2012a) *Human Development Index (HDI) – 2012 Rankings* [online] <http://hdr.undp.org/en/statistics/> [accessed 16 January 2014].

UNDP (2012b) *Malawi: Country Profile & Human Development Indicators* [online] <http://hdrstats.undp.org/en/countries/profiles/MWI.html> [accessed 16 January 2014].

UN-OHRLLS (2013) *Least Developed Countries: About LDCs* [online] <http://www.unohrlls.org/en/ldc/25/> [accessed 16 January 2014].

Appendix 6.1 Geographical scope of certification by product characteristics

Product category	Applicable to:	Product category	Applicable to:	Product category	Applicable to:
Almonds in shell	Pakistan (CP)	Apples	South Africa (conventional, SPO/HL), South America (C&O, SPO/HL)	Apples for drying	Eastern, Central and Western Asia (C&O, SPO), South America (organic, SPO), Pakistan (conventional, CP), South Africa (C&O, SPO/HL)
Apple Juice	South Africa (SPO/HL)	Apples for juice	Eastern, Central and Western Asia and South Africa (conventional organic, SPO/HL)	Apples for processing	Eastern, Central and Western Asia and South Africa (C&O, SPO/HL), South America (C&O, SPO/HL)
Banana	See original source (due to complexity)	Dates for drying	Tunisia and Egypt (C&O, SPO)	Fonio (C&O)	Western Africa (SPO)
Grapefruit	Mexico, South Africa, Northern Africa (C&O, SPO/HL)	Lemons	Argentina (C, SPO/HL), Egypt (C&O, SPO/HL), South Africa	Lemons for processing	Peru (O, SOP/HL)
Limes	Brazil (C, SPO/HL), Dominican Republic (O, SPO/HL), Caribbean, Egypt Mexico, Western Africa (C&O, SPO/HL)	Lychees	Eastern Africa, Southern Africa (C&O, SPO/HL)	Lychees for processing	Eastern Africa (C&O, SPO/HL)
Mangoes	Thailand (C, SPO/HL, Nam Dok Mai variety only), Central America, Caribbean, South America, South Africa (C&O, SPO/HL)	Mangoes for processing	Southern Asia, Western Africa, Eastern Africa, South-east Asia (C&O, SPO/HL), Peru (O, SPO/HL)	Mangoes for drying	Southern Asia, Western Africa, Eastern Africa, South-east Asia (C&O, SPO)
Mangoes for juice	South America, Caribbean, Southern Asia, Eastern Africa, Western Africa, (C&O, SPO/HL), South-east Asia (C, SPO/HL)	Mangoes for pulp	Cuba, Brazil (C, SPO/HL), Western Africa (C&O, SPO/HL)	Marula for processing	Africa (C&O, SPO)

Nectarines	Argentina (C, SPO/HL), Southern Africa (C&O, SPO/HL)	Oranges	Argentina, Egypt (C&O, SPO/HL), Morocco, South Africa (C, SPO/HL)	Oranges for processing	Peru (O, SPO/HL)
Papaya	Brazil, Eastern Africa (C&O, SPO/HL)	Papaya for juice	Eastern Africa (C&O, SPO/HL)	Papaya for drying	Eastern Africa (C&O, SPO)
Papayas for processing	Peru (O, SPO/HL)	Passion fruit for juice	Eastern Africa, South America, Eastern Africa, South-eastern Asia (C&O, SPO/HL)	Passion fruits for processing	South America, South-eastern Asia (C&O, SPO/HL)
Peaches	Argentina, Southern Africa (C, SPO/HL), Southern Africa (C&O, SPO/HL)	Pears	South Africa (C, SPO/HL), South America (C&O, SPO/HL)	Pears for drying	South America (C&O, SPO)
Pears for juice	South America (C&O, SPO/HL)	Pears for processing	South America (C&O, SPO/HL)	Pineapples incl. for processing	Eastern Africa, Western Africa, Middle Africa, South America, South-eastern Asia, Southern Asia, Caribbean (C&O, SPO/HL)
Pineapples for drying	Eastern Africa, Middle Africa, South-eastern Asia, Southern Asia, Caribbean, Western Africa except Ghana (C&O, SPO), Ghana (C&O, SPO/HL)	Plantains incl. for processing	Central America, South America (C, SPO/HL)	Plums	South Africa (C, SPO/HL)
Quinoa	South America (C&O, SPO)	Rice	Egypt (C&O, SPO)	Rice, Black and White 'petit poussin'	Laos (C, SPO)
Rice, glutinous (white)	Laos (C, SPO)	Rice, Mandarin (conventional)	Laos (SPO)	Rice, normal long grain (C&O)	Benin (SPO)

(Continue)

Appendix 6.1 Geographical scope of certification by product characteristics (*Continued*)

Product category	Applicable to:	Product category	Applicable to:	Product category	Applicable to:
Rice, traditional varieties from Sri Lanka	Sri Lanka (O, SPO)	Rice (conventional & organic)	India (CP), Pakistan (SPO), Thailand (SPO)	Seed cotton (C&O)	South America, Central America, Northern Africa, Eastern Africa, Western Africa, Middle Africa (all SPO), Southern Asia (SPO/ C)
Soft citrus	Argentina, South Africa (C, SPO/HL), Northern Africa (C&O, SPO/HL)	Table grapes	Egypt, Namibia, South Africa, Chile, Central America (C&O, SPO/HL), India (C, SPO/HL)	Wine grapes	South Africa, North Africa, South America, Georgia Lebanon (C&O, SPO/HL)
Walnut	Central Asia, South America (C&O, SPO), Pakistan (O, SPO)	Argan oil	Morocco (C&O, SPO)	Coconut	Windward Islands, South America, West Africa (C, SPO/HL)
Coconut for drying	Worldwide except Oceania (C&O, SPO)	Coconuts for processing	Worldwide except Oceania (C&O, SPO/HL), Oceania (C&O, SPO)	Shea butter	Western, Eastern and Middle Africa (C&O, SPO)
Apricots, dried	Pakistan (C&O, CP)	Mangoes, dried	Western Africa except Ghana (C&O, SPO), Ghana (C&O, SPO/HL)	Papaya, dried	Eastern Africa (C&O, SPO)
Passion fruit juice	South America (C&O, SPO/HL)	Pineapples, dried	Togo (O, SPO)	Dried plums	World Wide (C&O, SPO), South Africa (C&O, SPO/HL)
Raisin	South Africa (O, SPO), Southern Asia, Central Asia, South America (C&O, SPO)	Tomatoes, dried	Burkina Faso (C, SPO)	Wild Apricots, dried	Pakistan (C, CP)

Note: Abbreviations show types of standards that are available: C = contract, O = organic; SPO = small producer organization, HL = hired labour

Source: data from Fairtrade International, 2011a

CHAPTER 7

Fairtrade, sustainability standards, and the informal economy: What role for hired labourers?

Valerie Nelson and David Phillips

Abstract

Informality is a growing phenomenon in the global economy, and particularly evident when focusing on the circumstances of hired labour in rural areas of the global South. This article explores the relationship between Fairtrade and sustainability standards, and the informal economy. Recognizing that informal and formal economies are closely intertwined, the chapter focuses upon previously neglected value chain actors – casual workers employed by independent smallholders and outgrowers attached to formal enterprises in Fairtrade and certified global value chains. Analysing the changing terms of integration of these groups in dynamic global value chains provides standards organizations with an opportunity to reflect upon, and potentially improve their practice. Recognition of the basic labour rights and livelihood priorities of informal workers, as well as the myriad institutional arrangements which connect them to formal economies, is an important first step in identifying practical strategies for change.

Keywords: Fairtrade, informal, hired labour, value chains, sustainability

THERE HAS BEEN A RAPID expansion of Voluntary Sustainability Standard (VSS) systems in agricultural commodity markets in recent years (Potts et al., 2014; Byerlee and Rueda, 2015). This expansion has affected increasing numbers of farming systems and rural societies, triggering significant critical analysis and discussion with regard to issues of governance (Tallontire et al., 2011) and their social, political, and economic impacts (e.g. Raynolds, 2012; Cramer et al., 2016; Nelson and Martin, 2012, 2013, 2014). However, there has been limited attention given to the hired labour employed by smallholder farmers in certified value chains and those incorporated in global value chains through different kinds of outgrower arrangements.

In this chapter we explore the issue of hired labour on smallholder farms and outgrower schemes in certified value chains, particularly in the Fairtrade context. Analysing the terms of integration and assumptions concerning hired labour or informal workers within sustainability standards such as Fairtrade

http://dx.doi.org/10.3362/9781780449067.007

provides an opportunity for these organizations to reflect upon and potentially improve their practice.

To clarify terminology used in the chapter, the term 'Fairtrade International' refers to 'all or any part of the activities of FLO eV, FLO-CERT, Fairtrade producer networks, national Fairtrade organizations and Fairtrade marketing organizations. Fairtrade is used to denote the product certification system operated by Fairtrade International (FLO) (Fair Trade, 2011b). As opposed to the 'Fair Trade' movement, which is: 'the combined efforts of Fair Trade organizations, campaigners and businesses to promote and activate the Fair Trade principles of empowering producers, making trade more fair, and sustainable livelihoods' (Fair Trade, 2011b).

The sustainability standards that are members of ISEAL aim to be credible standards in the market place, assuring companies and producers that their tools and processes deliver fair and sustainable products. In light of this aim, in this chapter we explore sustainability standard credibility with respect to informal rural workers working for smallholder farmers, and hired labour in outgrower schemes. We review relevant impact studies on Fairtrade, but also to identify the extent to which the differentiated effects of Fairtrade and other standards are being fully addressed. We highlight the neglect of this particularly marginalized group within the standards and certification processes relating to agricultural value chains, and explore the reasons. We conclude by identifying future research priorities and possible strategies for action.

Informal economy

To begin an exploration of formal versus informal economy distinctions and concepts this section analyses the evolving academic and policy literature on informality as a guide to analysing the reach (or lack of) of Fairtrade and sustainability standards into the informal sector.

The concept of the informal economy was popularized by the social anthropologist Keith Hart in 1973 in an article entitled: 'Informal income opportunities and urban employment in Ghana'. There are varying schools of thought on informality, and there has been a distinct lack of clarity in definitions (Guha-Khasnobis et al., 2007). Martha Alter Chen (2007) defines the informal economy as including self-employment in unregulated, informal enterprises, as well as wage employment in informal jobs, which are not regulated but could be linked to a formally registered enterprise. An example of the latter would be situations in which casual workers are employed on South African fruit farms. For Guha-Khasnobis et al. (2007) the formal/informal economy divide can be critiqued, but it is here to stay and can be useful for analysis. They suggest that the reach of governance and level of structuring are the two dimensions of any economic activity that should be analysed. It is important not to assume, for example, that the informal sector is necessarily chaotic and unstructured; this is not always the case and such assumptions have led to inappropriate policy choices in the past (Guha-Khasnobis et al., 2007). Locally tailored, context-specific approaches are needed according to several current scholars (see Guha-Khasnobis et al., 2007; Lewis, 2016) to develop appropriate policies and programming. Formalization should not necessarily be assumed to be the only pathway forwards for the informal economy, and where it is locally appropriate steps should be designed with the informal economy in mind (Lewis, 2016).

Globally, there is an increasing level of informality in work. For instance, the ILO finds that more than '60% of all workers currently lack an employment contract, with most of them engaged in own-account or contributing family work in the developing world. However, even among wage and salaried workers, less than half (42 per cent) are working on a permanent contract' (ILO, 2015). Guy Standing outlines the makings of a new class, the 'precariat' – an emerging class of people around the world who are experiencing increasing levels of insecurity and unstable, low paid labour (Standing, 2016).

Research has shown that different patterns of employment can be associated with plantations and estates. In Tamil Nadu, Nilgiri Hills, labour shortages on tea plantations are occurring as the working population ages and their children have found more desirable jobs, for example in the textile sector in the lowlands, leading the tea estate managers to recruit migrant workers from the north of India while some have increased their sourcing from outgrower smallholders (Nelson and Martin, 2013). In the South African fruit industry there has been a process of 'casualization' of the labour force (an increase in casual, temporary, and part-time work in employment relationships) and externalization (where part of the work is outsourced to external contractors or agents under a commercial contract), although statistics are unreliable and there is a blurring of the lines: workers categorized as being in the informal or formal economy may each display characteristics of work commonly associated with the other (Devey et al., 2007). In contrast, in the Kenyan cut flower industry there has been a growing emphasis on permanent work with vocational training and worker welfare initiatives to improve worker skills to raise productivity and product quality, and so delivering greater continuity of production in a sector where inter-seasonal variation has reduced (Riisgaard and Gibbon, 2014). These wider labour market, industry, and demographic trends all play a key role in shaping the overall nature of an economy and sector and the relative levels of formality and informality seen within it.

Urban livelihoods rely substantially in developing countries upon informal activities such as home-based work, street vending, and collecting waste (Lewis, 2016). In rural areas the informal economy plays a vital role in agricultural development in sub-Saharan Africa, although policies have tended to favour large-scale investors and commercial operations (Vorley et al., 2012). Lewis (2016) emphasizes the scale, but also diversity of the rural informal economy, which includes trade, farming, crafts, services, construction, production and mining, and the fact that for some households the informal economy can provide an additional or 'secondary' stream of income or form part of a diversified household livelihood strategy (Lewis, 2016). Informal economic activities can also be 'a substitute for the lack of state protection' (Lewis, 2016: 21). Subsistence farmers are not classed as part of the informal economy, but smallholders who informally trade with different local and urban markets and contract farmers who sell produce informally to supplement their incomes are part of the informal economy (Lewis, 2016). There are also people, including migrants, who work for smallholders and outgrowers, conducting casual work to sustain a living, being paid in kind or in cash.

Policy prescriptions for the informal economy have in the past encouraged formalization, without adequate context-specific analysis (Guha-Khasnobis et al., 2007). Current policy discourse emphasizes participatory approaches, building upon existing community-level institutions, and appropriate design of policy or programme interventions to increase formalization in a set of steps. To support rural informal sectors, investments should be targeted beyond large-scale and formal enterprises, greater representation for those active in the informal sector should be facilitated, and ways found to avoid exclusion of informal workers from green growth strategies (Lewis, 2016). Recognition of such groups in policy-making is vital, but real incentives and simple procedures are needed for success (Lewis, 2016). For example, in Ethiopia the government has recognized artisanal and small-scale miners through legal changes, administrative modifications improving the issuing of licences, and improved access to extension services. In Colombia self-organization by workers has enabled them to gain bargaining power and recognition in policy (Lewis, 2016).

Terms of integration in global value chains

Earlier value chain studies focused upon the linkages between global buyers and local suppliers, distinguishing between diverse kinds of producers, but providing an inadequate analysis of labour (Bolwig et al., 2008).

An analytical framework provided by Bolwig et al. (2008: 2–3) can support a 'detailed and locally nuanced understanding of the internal structure and composition of livelihoods with the broader political economy within which they are situated, and the transnational linkages and networks that exist along a value chain'. Their framework includes an analysis of the (changing) position of specific chain actors, but also the terms of that participation. For some actors they may be excluded completely from a value chain as it changes in nature. The terms of participation for chain actors can also be dynamic – being weakened or strengthened through: a) top down requirements (e.g. changes in chain structure and governance, or the introduction of standards and certifications); or b) changes in the bottom up agency exerted by actors (Bolwig et al., 2008: 2). Moving beyond a management competence lens, Bolwig et al. (2008) also emphasize the limited power that small enterprises and farmers in developing countries often have to change their terms of integration in value chains vis-à-vis the power of actors downstream (e.g. importers and retailers). The terms of inclusion can be highly disadvantageous and careful cost-benefit analysis is necessary to understand the poverty implications of value chain processes (Bolwig et al., 2008). While social groups may be entirely integrated into specific global value chains, they may be marginalized based upon identity with limited recognition of their citizenship, for instance migrant Dalits working as agricultural labourers in India and African migrant workers picking fruit in South Africa (Bolwig et al., 2008).

The changing nature of global value chains is also emphasized by Barrientos et al. (2011) who have questioned the extent to which any moves by firms and workers from low to high value activities in global production networks lead to improved employment, rights, and protections for poorer producers and workers.

Vertical and horizontal intersections

In academic analysis of value chains there are both traditional analyses of value chains from a vertical perspective (for example mapping flows of Fairtrade goods from producer to consumer) and horizontal analyses that introduce social and political perspectives in a complementary or intersecting manner. As discussed in the preceding section, understanding and researching the intersection of vertical value chain and place-based horizontal dynamics and the potential and limits of Fairtrade and sustainability standards is important from a development perspective.

New research has highlighted how there has been a shift in recent years from traditional territorial forms of land governance, such as government land-use regulations and planning and community land management, to 'flow-centred arrangements', the latter referring to governance targeting particular flows of resources or goods, such as certification of agricultural or wood products (Sikor et al., 2013). Similar observations regarding a shift in the locus of power across scales, away from the local, as a result of processes of economic globalization and attendant ethical and sustainability standards, and codes in agriculture and forest-related commodities, have been explored by Otto Hospes (2014), Tallontire et al. (2011), Nelson and Tallontire (2014), and Nelson et al. (2014), who dissect politics and multi-scale governance processes in Kenyan-UK agrifood chains.

Neilson and Pritchard (2010) analyse the regional dynamics of fair and ethical trade in plantation zones of South India. Earlier studies such as that by Nelson et al. (2000) compared conventional and ethical trading of Ecuadorian cocoa and Brazil nuts in Peru, to seek to unpack the institutional and livelihood contexts in which fair and ethical trade schemes are implemented (see also Nelson et al., 2002). This research found that certain social groups in the value chain were not able to participate (porters and shellers of Brazil nuts), and instead the Brazil nut concession holders were the ones to participate and capture benefits, albeit of a limited nature.

Neilson and Pritchard promote 'a "horizontal analysis" which understands fair and ethical trade as a set of *introduced* discourses and practices within producer communities that are already institutionally embedded within particular sociospatial environments' (Neilson and Pritchard, 2010: 1834). They argue that while such schemes can deliver benefits to individuals, as standards operate in embedded contexts, there are implications and consequences that cannot always be recognized or anticipated. Their work cites cases of South Indian tea and coffee, where fair and ethical trade does not engage with the most important socio-economic problems, namely the issue of plantation abandonment in Kerala and the *de facto* exclusion of smallholders from the reach of sustainability standards. This uneven implementation of sustainability standards and their lack of attention to regional economic and governance institutions are problematic from a development perspective (Neilson and Pritchard, 2010).

We suggest that it is important to understand the current scope of Fairtrade and other sustainability standards to help identify their limitations and their potential (including new opportunities to reach disadvantaged groups) and to better delineate appropriate complementary or alternative initiatives. This can be done through a horizontal analysis which intersects with place-based labour geographies and production networks.

Fairtrade inclusion and exclusion thresholds

Fairtrade has inclusion and exclusion thresholds, because a certain level of assets is needed, such as land, to participate in Fairtrade (Nelson and Pound, 2009). In this context it is necessary to explore how workers in the informal economy participate in value chains that are certified to Fairtrade and/or other sustainability standards. We review impact studies to identify: a) whether there is empirical evidence on hired labourers and informal work in relevant impact studies; and b) what the empirical evidence says about the benefits and costs incurred by such casual workers who are integrated into global value chains that are certified to Fairtrade or other sustainability standards. Theoretically speaking, informal workers could be employed by smallholders in certified producer organizations, or they could be employed by smallholders who themselves are contract farmers for certified plantations, or they could work informally for Fairtrade-certified estates.

Studies on the impacts of Fairtrade and other sustainability standards have increased in number in recent years and collectively have begun to show the *highly context-specific* nature of sustainability standard outcomes. This is unsurprising, because sustainability standards and Fairtrade are adopted by producer groups and estates that are already embedded in rural societies, each with its own place-specific political economy.

Individuals who provide casual labour for smallholders in certified value chains can be termed informal workers. Informal workers are also those who may be engaged by enterprises associated with formal estates or plantations. We assess the visibility and recognition of this group in Fairtrade thinking and literature and analyse their terms of participation. In a sense these workers are at the bottom end of what can be long value chains and a question arises as to whether their participation in such chains can be considered 'fair' and 'sustainable'.

We review the issue of hired labour and informality with respect to different agricultural sustainability standards, particularly Fairtrade International (FLO), henceforth referred to as Fairtrade. Fairtrade has social justice aims and takes actions on standards compliance management, Fairtrade Premium expenditure, and workers' rights. Fairtrade offers producers opportunities to operate in export markets on better terms, delivering benefits to those involved in producing export agriculture crops such as coffee, cocoa, tea, sugar, and bananas (see FLO, 2011c). In seeking to advance conditions for workers in agriculture value chains, Fairtrade aims to improve standards of employment and worker well-being, labour rights, and empowerment (FLO, 2011a).

At the same time, we suggest that Fairtrade has development ambitions, and that any development organization or intervention will likely have differentiated impacts and could potentially increase inequalities without due consideration of local social relations. It is therefore important to explore who is participating in Fairtrade, beyond the most obvious target group of smallholder producers and permanent workers in formal labour contexts, and whether they are benefiting or experiencing costs. Just as the gender impacts of Fairtrade have been analysed (Kasente, 2012), the broader social difference dimensions of impact need to be unpacked and taken into account. As with gendered impacts, interventions risk further marginalizing already vulnerable groups if they ignore the wider range of social discriminations in the contexts within which they play out.

Fairtrade has its origins in a solidarity movement based upon civic conventions, but has moved towards industrial conventions much more focused upon the market (Renard, 2003; Raynolds et al., 2007; Raynolds, 2014; Riisgard and Gibbon, 2014; Riisgard, 2015). As a market-based mechanism there are limits to what may be perceived as the responsibility of Fairtrade to influence. We contend that the boundary of what is considered *material* (in the language of corporate responsibility) to Fairtrade producer organizations and estates is expanding – both in the perception of external stakeholders, but also internally within Fairtrade. As discussed in the preceding section, understanding and researching the intersection of vertical value chain and place-based horizontal dynamics and the potential and limits of Fairtrade and sustainability standards is important from a development perspective.

Methodology

Our analysis relies upon a systematic analysis of the findings from a number of empirical impact assessments conducted by the authors and colleagues at the Natural Resources Institute to understand if and how informal workers engage in global value chains or are excluded and the terms of their integration.[1] We also analyse the quality of the evidence available. Further, we have reviewed relevant literature using a snowball approach, identifying new studies through our personal research networks.

We analyse the position and terms of integration of informal workers in certified global value chains in order to assess the existing evidence base and to identify potential action strategies for Fairtrade and voluntary sustainability standards and other actors in reaching more marginal groups. Gender and social difference approaches and analytical frameworks also provide tools for unpacking the processes within which Fairtrade is adopted by producers (see Nelson and Martin, 2013), and the terms upon which the latter are integrated into global value chains (Riisgaard et al., 2010).

The intersection between the vertical value chain and horizontal rural governance is the space in which smallholders may capture an increased share of value in lucrative, but potentially risky, global value chains. We seek evidence on these intersections in the literature.

Analysing the terms of integration for informal workers in global value chains supports an analysis of processes of accumulation and loss, of costs and benefits, and of risks and opportunities. This should enable sustainability standards organizations to reflect upon the inherent assumptions within their theories of change to improve their practice and support the generation of an evidence base.

The context of dynamic rural economies

Certified value chains are embedded in a wide range of highly diverse labour markets and rural societies, many of which are also changing rapidly. Key rural stressors include land fragmentation through inheritance processes, large-scale acquisitions, and agricultural investments; growing population and exodus to urban centres (especially male outmigration); and multiple demands on agriculture from an environmental sustainability perspective and food security. Policy levers in sub-Saharan Africa tend to be biased towards large-scale agriculture, despite the fact that smallholders are the biggest investors in agriculture (Vorley et al., 2012). There are also growing opportunities in domestic, regional, and international trade.

While many rural societies face these challenges, it is also important to recognize that the dynamics of rural economies and labour markets are *highly context specific*, with variability in environmental endowments and entitlements and social relations (Nelson and Martin, 2012). The type of hired labour arrangements will also, therefore, vary by place. Smallholders and other rural groups are incorporated into and engage with value chains – local, domestic, and international – on different terms (Riisgaard et al., 2010) depending upon their bargaining power, which itself is shaped by local history, culture, and social constructions. This is also the case for the rural dwellers who are employed occasionally or regularly as hired labourers by smallholders. Within this dynamic picture of rural economies labour markets are also rapidly changing.

Global agricultural trade has significantly increased in recent decades, especially in higher value products where food quality and sustainability standards
are important (e.g. fruit, vegetables, seafood, fish, meat, and dairy products)
with the most marked shift to higher value exports in developing countries
(FAO, 2015). There is increasing 'vertical integration, upgrading of the supply
base and increased dominance of large multinational food companies' (FAO,
2015: 2). These changes offer opportunities for generating rural employment
and tackling poverty, but the increasing stringency of product and production
standards may have exclusionary effects on smallholders in contract farming schemes (FAO, 2015). Vorley et al. (2012: 9) suggest that more attention
needs to be paid to the differentiation in rural worlds which is resulting from
processes of globalization. While large producers in the top level are able to
compete globally, those in the middle level have access to land but may be
undercapitalized and affected by declining terms of trading. At the bottom
sit those with fragile livelihoods and limited access to productive resources,
sometimes including multi-occupational migrants and unskilled, uneducated
people dependent on low-waged, casual family labour (Vorley, 2002: 9).

Changing expectations of Fairtrade

Expectations of what Fairtrade seeks to deliver are being made clearer with
the development and publication of an organizational theory of change based
upon a process of stakeholder participation. Societal expectations of Fairtrade
are changing, as are the expectations of Fairtrade stakeholders. Prior to this,
Nelson and Martin (2013) had also used theory-based evaluation to assess the
poverty impact of voluntary standards, including Fairtrade and Rainforest Alliance, and this involved articulating hypothetical theories of change, which
were then used to guide data collection and analysis to assess effectiveness
and impact. Impact studies and analyses of Fairtrade have helped to clarify
what Fairtrade actually is in terms of its theory of change and Fairtrade itself
has now invested in a participatory process of theory of change formulation.

Fairtrade does not purport to *solve* issues such as poverty, gender inequality, and environmental degradation. In a 2009 meta-review of the evidence on
the impact of Fairtrade, conducted by the Natural Resources Institute for the
Fairtrade Foundation, we recognized that Fairtrade, as a market mechanism,
is not expecting or seeking to solve rural poverty, but we also raised questions
regarding its contribution: 'Fairtrade does not claim to solve rural poverty
in developing countries, but if helping poor households to tackle poverty is
the ultimate objective of Fairtrade then it is reasonable to explore how far
Fairtrade is achieving this in different situations' (Nelson and Pound, 2009:
6). Further more, we noted that Fairtrade's 'ability to raise [poor] producers
out of poverty is an important part of its credibility in the marketplace and
with donors' (Nelson and Pound, 2009: 39). Our impact assessment of voluntary sustainability standards (Nelson and Martin, 2013) found limits to the
effectiveness of such initiatives and identified the need for complementary

approaches to reach more marginal groups and to tackle more structural issues that create poverty.

The new *Fairtrade Theory of Change* (TOC) (Fairtrade International, 2015: 6–7) articulates the following goals as desired impacts, to which Fairtrade makes a contribution. These are goals of 'Make Trade Fair; Empower Small Producers and Workers; and Foster Sustainable Livelihoods'. Fairtrade's vision is 'a world in which all small producers and workers can enjoy secure and sustainable livelihoods, fulfil their potential and decide on their future' (Fairtrade International, 2016). While Fairtrade cannot solve such challenges, it is necessary, particularly where such schemes receive donor support, that Fairtrade understands its responsibilities in the rural milieu (Nelson and Martin, 2013).

Different impact pathways are identified in the overall Fairtrade theory of change. The specific impact pathway that focuses on trade leads to the goal of 'Making Trade Fair'. There are two routes to achieving fairer trade – firstly, achieving fairer trade *within* Fairtrade supply chains, but also more broadly achieving *systemic change* in the way trade is practised and regulated (Fairtrade International, 2016). Fairtrade acknowledges that such systemic level change, i.e. changing global trade, cannot be achieved by Fairtrade alone, recognizing that the sphere of influence of Fairtrade has limits, but also clarifying the contribution that Fairtrade could make in this regard. What is needed is:

> A broad coalition of actors working towards common goals, progressive business (including Fair Trade businesses) spearheading fair and sustainable trading practices and acting as vocal advocates within their industries and with policy makers; and political leadership within national governments and regional and global institutions (Fairtrade International, 2015: 27).

The ability of Fairtrade to change practices on a systemic level is shaped, in part, by its market success, with the latter conferring credibility upon and leveraging influence by Fairtrade. But at the same time, progress is needed on broader systemic issues such as agreement on living wages, to enable Fairtrade to make trade fair in its own supply chains (ibid.).

While Fairtrade has publicly recognized the role of trade in shaping inequality, it is not always clear how it seeks to mitigate or avoid such outcomes. We suggest that Fairtrade should have greater awareness of the differentiated nature of rural societies, *including informal workers,* which can be facilitated through impact evaluations and stakeholder learning processes in specific localities or landscapes. Enhanced recognition of informal workers is a first step to strengthening their bargaining power (Lewis, 2016) and is thus relevant to sustainability standards and particularly Fairtrade. National and regional producer networks and producer participation in Fairtrade governance are unique aspects of Fairtrade. However, do these networks represent diverse rural worlds? Do they give recognition to the informal workers that are participating in global value chains including certified ones?

Informal work and Fairtrade certification

Fairtrade originated as a form of solidarity trade involving Latin American coffee smallholders. In contrast to many other voluntary sustainability standards, such as Rainforest Alliance and Utz Certified, whose early emphasis has been on certifying larger farms and sometimes associated outgrowers, the prime focus of Fairtrade International continues to be smallholder farmers and farmer organizations. However, the members of these organizations tend to be those that own land and have access to assets (Blowfield et al., 1999). This is reflected in the extensive literature that has focused on Fairtrade certification of smallholder producers and their organizations in different country and commodity contexts, but less study of formal plantations and hired labour situations, contract farming and very little about the situation of informal workers working on smallholder farms as one of many livelihood strategies or in other more complex outgrower relationships.

The lack of available literature identified that addresses issues of informal workers and labour is striking. There are few studies which consider this issue and most include only fragmentary evidence. In this section we explore the limited number of case studies that we did find and aim to synthesize the main insights that this literature presents. This is not intended as a systematic review of the evidence base, but the analysis serves to elucidate some of the issues arising for this marginal group, who have been neglected in the vast majority of impact studies to date.

Tea

In 2009 a review of the evidence base on the impact of Fairtrade highlighted the lack of study of hired labour situations (Nelson and Pound, 2009). More recently, studies have investigated Fairtrade adoption and impact in contexts of permanent employees on plantations, for example, in tea, (Dolan, 2008, 2010; Makita, 2012), and cut flowers and bananas (Riisgaard and Gibbon, 2014; Riisgaard and Hammer, 2014; Raynolds, 2012). In contrast, hired labourers who are employed by smallholder farmers or on outgrower schemes or informal workers in estates/plantations have been relatively invisible in certified agricultural value chain studies and debates.

In Kenyan tea, Stathers et al. (2013) studied the poverty impact of Voluntary Sustainability Standards, including Fairtrade and Rainforest Alliance. They found that most of the hired labourers plucking green leaf on smallholder tea farms are neighbouring tea farmers who engage in paid plucking work in between the weekly plucking rounds on their own farms. However, there are also hired labourers who come from more distant areas and who may live with their host farmer (Stathers et al., 2013). For migrants the challenges and hardships may vary, as compared with those who conduct work on a neighbours' farm. Many of the hired labourers are female pluckers, who top up their farming income with work on their neighbours' farms. Gender discrimination with respect to access to land and participation in farmer associations and groups (Stathers et al., 2013) essentially shapes the participation of women in the tea value chain, with some having to supplement their income or rely on casual labour in order to secure their livelihoods.

In a study of poverty impacts of sustainability standards in tea in the Nilgiris district, India, worker terms and conditions and environmental practices on certified and non-certified farms were compared. Several certified farms held Rainforest Alliance certification, and some of them also held other certifications, such as Utz Certified and in one case Fairtrade. A comparison was made with an estate selling on to domestic markets, which did not hold any sustainability certifications. Managers across the sector in the Nilgiris are facing labour shortages, because of the ageing population and outmigration of youth to more attractive jobs in textiles and information technology (IT) industries in the lowlands. Public construction work opportunities also offer higher wages which tempts workers and raises absenteeism levels. Managers are resorting to bringing in migrant labour from the north of India to conduct the plucking work on the estates. As the in-migrants do not represent a threat to the jobs of existing workers, relations between migrants and the pre-existing local workforce have been relatively cordial. However, more research is needed to understand the situation for the young, mainly female migrant workers who are recruited in the north of India and brought to work in Tamil Nadu. Workers, both established and newer migrants, interviewed in focus group discussions on the Joint Body at the Fairtrade estate were positive about the opportunity the Joint Body had presented to them to engage with management, but there was a certain lack of clarity regarding decision-making on the use of the premium funds.

Makita (2012) also analysed management–worker relations on an Indian tea plantation and found that workers experienced benefits from Fairtrade certification, but had limited knowledge of Fairtrade and how it works, especially how the Joint Body which is established to *represent* them was funded. Makita (2012) concludes that the 'invisibility' of Fairtrade among many workers unintentionally reinforced (hierarchical) patron–client relations that characterized management–worker relations. At the time of the study in India by Nelson et al. (2009–13) in the Nilgiris, the smallholder sector had not yet been reached by Rainforest Alliance, Fairtrade, or Utz Certified, except for a few outgrowers associated with some of the estates, yet this is informal economy supports large numbers of rural households, which potentially hire informal workers themselves.

Sugar

Existing, often uneven, patterns of wealth and asset ownership form the context in which sustainability standards seek to regulate social and environmental conditions of production, and in the case of Fairtrade, fairness in the value chain. Various studies of Fairtrade and other sustainability standards provide insights into hired labour issues on smallholder or outgrower farms in the sugar sector and demonstrate how pre-existing patterns of wealth and inequality shape outcomes for chain actors, including the less well recognized informal workers and labourers. In research conducted on a Fairtrade sugar scheme in Malawi, Phillips (2014) found that sites of uneven access to land and wealth (both within the scheme and prevailing embedded rural governance) unintentionally led to more instances of exclusion and inequalities. In this particular scheme land titles were held by farmers who represented approximately one-third of the membership of the outgrower scheme. However, the majority of the work conducted in the field was in fact carried out by a mixture of permanent and seasonal hired labour.

Some permanent employees participated in matters related to Fairtrade (for example two employees joined the Fairtrade Premium Committee). However, the majority of employees and hired labour reported exclusion and marginalization from anything related to Fairtrade certification, and therefore did not experience the same financial and capacity building experiences of many of the farmers and management teams. Thus, despite participation in the Fairtrade certified value chain, the role of certain groups in the production of sugar was not being specifically recognized by the sustainability standard and so there was no opportunity for them to improve their bargaining power and terms of integration into the value chain. Indeed, risks of further marginalization may arise when social groups are overlooked in this way. On the positive side, it is possible that Fairtrade certification could improve the viability of the outgrower scheme and have a knock on effect on the amount of work available for those conducting casual labour, but more research would be needed to ascertain whether this is indeed the case.

For employees, including informal employees on plantations, estates, and processing factories, and those working as casual labourers on smallholder farms, historical institutional factors influence sector dynamics, value chain relations, and their terms of integration. Various scholars have noted the influence of colonial and post-colonial legacies in shaping relations between the members of farmer groups and schemes and in industrial relations on plantations. Nelson and Martin (2012, 2015) explore such issues in tea estates in India and in Kenya. Tallontire (2014: 372) finds that:

> The story of Fairtrade in Africa is shaped by institutional structures such as the role of farmer organizations, particularly the role of cooperatives, and marketing structures, which in many African countries are part of its colonial legacy, as well as patterns of landholding (including the balance of large-scale commercial and smallholder farming) and social relations related to ethnicity and gender.

Nelson and Martin identify producer organization governance and history as a key element in shaping Fairtrade impacts (Nelson and Martin, 2013, 2014). Similarly, Stevis (2015) notes, Fairtrade is operating in and trying to socially regulate dispersed workplaces shaped by historical global production networks. Such historical contexts influence contemporary sites of, among other things, elite capture, patrimonial relations, patronage, dependencies, and subordination as evidenced from descriptions of plantation owners as 'the king of the estate and the father of the workers' (Makita, 2012: 94) or notions of 'them and us' between farmer landowners and workers (Phillips, 2014).

In a lot of Fairtrade discourse and marketing there is often an uncontested representation of the 'producer'. This is often demonstrated by the use of images of a smallholder farmer as an example of a producer who is marginalized from participation in and benefits from agriculture value chains, but also in the emphasis of the organization as a whole. While it is not disputed that thousands of smallholder farmers are just above or often below the poverty line, such representation obscures the differentiated nature of rural worlds (Nelson and Martin, 2013). In particular, the fact that there are often large numbers of employees and hired labour involved in the production of 'smallholder' produce is unrecognized.

In critical analysis of this invisibility of informal workers and labourers, Phillips (2014) explored an embedded social and political context in a production locality or place to reveal different categories of producers living uneven experiences in terms of Fairtrade certification in Malawi. Expanding upon Makita's (2012) categorization of employees as Management, Staff, Sub-staff, and Rank and File workers, the fourth category can be unpacked to highlight differences between, for example, permanent employees and hired seasonal (migrant) labour. He concludes that many categories of labour or worker have highly varied needs and experiences depending on their contractual arrangements, locations, and positionality.

Non-timber forest products

While not a sustainability standard, a study of a fair trading scheme in the early 2000s also highlighted how the role of specific social groups can be overlooked by those managing such schemes. In an early study of the comparative impact of conventional and ethical trading in Brazil nuts in Peru, Nelson et al. (2000) analysed a Fair Trade scheme. An association of Brazil nut concession holders in the Madre de Dios region of Peru were supported by a Peruvian NGO, with the latter supporting the concessionaires to trade their brazil nuts on fairer terms. However, the qualitative impact study found that porters were doing a large part of the arduous work of collecting Brazil nuts in the forest and transporting them to town. These porters and the shellers, largely female, were both ignored by the Fair Trade scheme, which engaged with and benefited the Brazil nut concessionaires only (Nelson et al., 2000).

Coffee

In a study of the impacts of Fairtrade on coffee farmers, cooperatives, and labourers in Nicaragua, Valkila and Nygren (2010) found that most producers had limited awareness of Fairtrade rules regarding working conditions on coffee farms. In a context of underemployment, a general practice of offering any work at any wage rate was considered sufficient. By neglecting requirements of fair working conditions, the working conditions on certified farms did not differ from typical informal working conditions in rural Nicaragua. In other words, the terms of integration of those at the bottom of the value chain were not affected.

As many coffee cooperatives have grown, investment in processing has also increased. The study by Valkila and Nygren (2010) also found that workers employed in Fairtrade certified processing plants received no additional benefits such as medical care as a result of certification. While premiums were invested in the wider community, the workers processing coffee were not considered a target group to receive such funds and so missed out. The lack of evidence of significant enhancement of labour standards of coffee production and processing, according to the authors, suggests a need to look at hired labour standards in other commodities such as tea and bananas and introduce elements to Fairtrade coffee contexts where more labour is employed.

Cocoa

An impact evaluation of VSS (Rainforest Alliance, Fairtrade, and Utz) assessed the poverty impact of Fairtrade in Ghanaian cocoa and of various voluntary sustainability standards in Ecuadorian cocoa.[2] In Ghanaian cocoa, workers on smallholder farms can have differing relationships with the land owner. On the majority of cocoa farms (certified and non-certified) in the study sample, hired casual labourers were employed in cocoa production tasks. Much of this hired labour was drawn from the north of Ghana, i.e. migrants moving to other regions of the country to seek work in the cocoa sector. The costs of hired labour were rising at the time of the study, creating challenges for the smallholder farm owners. Different terms of integration into the value chain for migrant workers were found to exist. Few Fairtrade impacts were identified for 'caretaker' farmers who work for farm owners for a share of the crop (33–50 per cent) since they cannot be Producer Organization members in their own right and thus are not directly eligible for benefits. However, the study found a reported improvement through reduced exposure to health and safety hazards for hired labour in Ghana resulting from Fairtrade (Nelson et al., 2013).

In Ecuador, a study by Cepeda et al. (2013) found that more certified producers were hiring labour than non-certified producers for reasons that were unclear. While there were improvements achieved in conditions for labourers, these were actually found to have primarily been the result of government pressure leading to a rise in payments, improvements in health and safety, and a reduction in child labour, rather than by the voluntary sustainability standards (Nelson and Martin, 2013).

Cotton

While it would seem important that VSS recognize the often invisible informal workers in many global value chains, it is also relevant to ask what might constitute a reasonable expectation of what a VSS can achieve in terms of poverty impact as a non-market mechanism. A study of the early impacts of Better Cotton Initiative (BCI) adoption in Kurnool District of Andhra Pradesh (Kumar et al., 2015) demonstrates the far-reaching extent of casual work on smallholder farms mainly by women, and often children as well in cotton production in the area.[3] The BCI standard focuses its decent work requirements on preventing the worst forms of child labour and on preventing gender discrimination. An Indian non-governmental organization (NGO) is implementing a project supporting farmer capacity strengthening and organization with the aim of BCI mainstreaming in the sector. The baseline study shows, among other things, the significant importance of hired labour on smallholder farms in cotton production in this area to the livelihoods of individuals and households experiencing poverty (Kumar et al., 2015). Work in cotton production provides poorer people, particularly women and children, with the chance to earn additional income and as such is an important livelihood strategy.

An analysis of the theory of change of the BCI, as implemented in a project by an NGO, indicates that it may be difficult for the VSS and project partners to address issues of decent work given the embedded nature of these challenges within institutions, culture, and social relations in the area, the limited resources available, and the central focus on improving yields and reducing environmental impacts. Cotton farmers report that they are currently hiring labour from the local community, within the village and nearby villages (Kumar et al., 2015). During sowing, farmers usually hire local labour and during harvesting they hire both locally and from nearby villages. The BCI project is mandated to work on promoting enabling mechanisms relating to smallholder finance and market access for the farmers, but the challenges are significant. The baseline study shows how cotton farmers in Kurnool face indebtedness due to the trading relationships of tied finance that they have with intermediaries. Therefore, smallholders themselves have limited capacity to afford improvements in terms and conditions for their labourers in the near term, and in the longer term would need to realize substantial benefits in order to have the opportunity to improve working conditions for those that they hire to work on their farms.

From a gender standpoint, there is widespread and entrenched gender inequality. There appear to be widespread unequal pay structures between men and women: women and men are not paid the same rates when they work as hired labourers, provision of water for drinking and handwashing is also variable (which affects women who provide much of the labour in cotton harvesting), and women often have to bring young children with them to work. There is little recognition of women's rights with respect to education and land tenure (Kumar et al., 2015). Women have more limited access to education than their male counterparts, and are less involved in household decision-making. They have a greater work burden – in domestic and reproductive tasks as well as in farming.

In a four-country qualitative evaluation of Fairtrade's impact in cotton, Nelson and Smith (2011) found that in Mali there are traditional forms of mutual labour exchange, but such traditions are already changing and in some cases can be further challenged by the adoption of Fairtrade. Any development interventions, including market mechanisms, risk exacerbating existing processes of marginalization without careful analysis of who they are engaging with and with what consequences.

Discussion

Non-recognition of informal workers in certified value chains

Informal workers, particularly those hired by smallholders, are not adequately recognized as a chain actor by Fairtrade and sustainability standards. This group has been overlooked as they are not the immediate target of these standards. However, there is an opportunity to expand their impact by considering if such a group could be recognized, and a moral case to consider whether their interventions could exacerbate rural inequalities.

Empirical evidence is also lacking in impact studies with respect to the position and terms of integration of informal workers in Fairtrade and other certified value chains. Our review of a number of studies shows that more nuanced and in-depth research is needed on the issues facing informal workers in specific value chains as they are embedded in particular places. Frequently, consultancy evaluations for sustainability standards have to focus limited resources upon chain actors more directly targeted by the non-market mechanism in question. However, thematic studies could focus more directly on informal work in certified value chains.

Terms of incorporation into certified global value chains

Smallholder integration into global value chains has been explored by Riisgaard et al. (2010), who note the potential for adverse incorporation due to weak bargaining power. Analysing the terms of integration of overlooked chain actors is also important to understand the intended and unintended consequences of sustainability standards in certified value chains.

Existing social relations have an influence on the roles and power of different social groups in any particular place and in the value chains that are embedded there. Smith (2014) suggests that entrenched gender relations shape men's and women's, girls' and boys' livelihood opportunities in value chains, particularly global value chains, because of the gendered economy (Smith, 2014). Gender relations and other forms of discrimination interconnect (in processes known as 'intersectionality') and shape access to assets, such as land, capital, labour, and social networks, in turn influencing their capacity to participate in different value chains and to benefit from them. Women were more likely to be carrying out casual labour in the Indian BCI cotton study area and in the Kenyan tea study for their neighbours as part of a livelihood survival strategy. The agency of individuals and groups working collectively is also relevant in any social change process, and although no examples were found in the literature to demonstrate positive agency in improving informal workers' bargaining power, this could be because they were not being looked for. Fairtrade also often works with more remote groups of smallholders, and this means that they may be more likely to be affected by issues of spatial marginalization (such as remoteness from centres of power, or lacking in access to infrastructure).

The importance of horizontal analysis

The institutional arrangements by which informal workers are engaged in the value chain are varied and context-specific. The Malawi tea example shows how smallholders may participate in outgrower schemes, often associated with larger plantations or estates, but they may also engage hired labourers themselves for informal work. It is very common in the informal sector that smallholders pay hired labourers a piece rate or agree a daily wage arrangement, but there can be other institutional arrangements, such as sharecropping and caretaker farmer situations as seen in the cocoa industry in Ghana. Further, some workers are employed in non-financial arrangements, such as reciprocal labour arrangements or mutual labour exchange. This is more likely to involve individuals from neighbouring farms – who may also be growing the same crop, but adding to their income, participating in mutual labour sharing practices, or seeking casual local labour. Migrant workers may come from further afield on a seasonal or more permanent basis.

Local production practices and access to inputs will also influence the extent to which health and safety is an issue. Differences also flow from the nature of the commodity in question. Some crops, such as cotton, are produced in periodic or a single harvest and this is generally when most labour is required. In other commodities, the work may be more year-round, for instance, tea plucking. The production cycles of the specific crop thus influence labour requirements and how workers may or may not be pushed/pulled into casual work. Further, economic and labour market dynamics of supply and demand in a particular region influence the employment opportunities, wages, and conditions for hired labourers.

Informal worker agency and organization

Informal workers in rural areas, especially in remote regions, have limited negotiating power because of their lack of organization. The challenges for farm worker organization are well rehearsed in the literature, but these are particularly acute for temporary or seasonal workers, who tend to have less protection in the law, and especially for those employed by disadvantaged smallholders who have limited bargaining power and resources themselves.

While hired labourers working on smallholder farms tend to have fewer resources at their disposal compared with smallholder farmers, it is also the case that they are active agents in their own right. Hired labourers often hold information on the prices smallholders receive from producer organizations, and are sometimes able to negotiate agreements with their smallholder employers even in such informal settings and particularly in situations of labour shortages (Nelson et al., 2016).

There is frequently a difference between the bargaining power of workers if they are living locally, compared with the situation of migrant workers which can be more precarious. In Ghana, migrant sharecroppers working for cocoa smallholders may benefit from the arrangement, but they are not able to share in the benefits of Fairtrade certification (Nelson et al., 2013). More research is needed on the varying arrangements by which they are incorporated in global value chains, how they might better organize, and if/how smallholders can afford to treat them better.

Affordability for smallholders of making decent work improvements for informal employees

A key issue is the affordability for smallholders of making improvements to the terms and conditions of those working for them on their farms. Smallholders themselves vary hugely even within a specific country, but even more so globally, in terms of their knowledge, assets, and wealth (including income levels, but also income security). There is a stark difference, for example, between larger-scale banana growers in Latin America, compared with a smallholder tea producer in Tanzania with a small plot of land. Smallholders in many rural areas of developing countries are challenged by multiple and intersecting stressors, including a changing climate, population pressure, rising food insecurity, ageing populations, and outmigration. Many smallholders participating in local, national, and particularly global value chains face significant volatility and risks. Their starting point assets and wealth levels, plus spatial location (e.g. level of remoteness) and contextual drivers thus influence the affordability of their making improvements for employees.

Smallholders' capacity to make changes in this regard also relies on knowledge and skills, as well as issues of affordability. For example, it is important to consider not only wage levels and forms and timings of payments, but other issues such as contracts and health and safety measures which may be important for worker health and livelihood security. While it is clear that struggling smallholder farmers have limited ability to take action, there may be some areas where improvements could be made with additional support. For example, in Ghana some hired labourers on cocoa smallholder farms reported improvements in health and safety, because they had been advised of some basic precautions by Fairtrade cocoa farmers. They were not allowed to attend formal training sessions organized via the cooperative, because they do not hold land title and are not members of the cooperative, but a change of cooperative policy would seem an opportunity to reach beyond the membership at relatively low cost. Identifying such 'low hanging fruit' measures might extend the impact of Fairtrade and bring positive benefits for on-farm workers. Currently, however, there appears to be limited recognition of the chain actor and the issues they face.

The effectiveness of sustainability standards in realizing benefits for smallholders will partially determine whether the smallholders have the capacity to improve the terms and conditions for their labourers. In Fairtrade, benefits are generated for members in different ways, including the benefits from premium investments by their producer organization, and sometimes training in improving product quality and quantity and where organizational strengthening and improved export prices are captured by the producer organization and passed on to members. The capacity of the producer organization to do this depends on its history and current functionality. Other types of sustainability standards have differing combinations of mechanisms to effect change, but many seek to generate market premiums as well as improving agricultural productivity and quality and environmental sustainability, thus benefiting individual farmers. Market demand plays a key role in shaping the extent to which Fairtrade can have traction with producer organizations. For instance, the amount of the organization's product that will be sold on Fairtrade terms could potentially be realized as individual benefits for smallholders. There is mixed evidence on the effectiveness of Fairtrade in realizing benefits for such smallholders (Nelson and Martin, 2014).

Conclusion

Our analysis of a series of impact studies and associated literature on fair trade, Fairtrade, and sustainability standards indicates that informal workers are not being reached by many such initiatives. Informal workers have been somewhat invisible in Fairtrade thinking, because of the over-riding focus on particular target groups by such initiatives. By encouraging a horizontal analysis as well as a vertical one, impact and research studies can illuminate the role of neglected actors in the value chain or affected by it amid existing labour geographies and economic flows.

More research is needed to illuminate how people engage in informal work. There are multiple working arrangements in global value chains, including increased casual work in employment relationships, increased outsourcing of work using labour brokers, smallholders that hire locals or migrant workers to do temporary work, more long-term sharecropping arrangements between small and medium-size land owners and migrant workers, and outgrowers associated with formal enterprises who hire casual workers. Forms of remuneration and benefit-sharing also vary. There are clear gender and social difference dimensions to labour markets, which shape who is more likely to be undertaking such work. This diversity of institutional arrangements and the dynamic nature of value chains, industries, and labour markets should be better understood by sustainability standards and other development organizations.

We suggest that greater recognition is needed of informal work in Fairtrade value chains, because currently it tends to be invisible and so opportunities may be missed to support informal workers, and potential negative unintended impacts are not recognized. At the same time, if actions are taken to influence the terms of integration of informal workers in certified value chains, the potential exclusionary effects would need to be considered – in other words, if more demands are placed on smallholders, then sustainability standards would become even further out of reach than they already are for the more marginal smallholders and smallholder organizations that struggle to meet Fairtrade requirements. Smallholders themselves are incorporated into global export value chains with very limited bargaining power and so their room for manoeuvre is limited.

For smallholders to change their behaviour may require increased capability (e.g. knowledge and skills, resources) as well as internal motivation and a perceived opportunity. New knowledge and skills could be generated through a greater recognition in the first instance by Fairtrade of the existence and role of informal workers in the chain. The health and safety information sharing is an obvious example, but there could be others. Producer groups and Fairtrade training could be more proactive in ensuring that informal workers can participate in training or receive information. However, it is also important to recognize that resources may be needed as well as a culture shift if smallholders and informal workers are to be able to change their behaviour, e.g. using personal protective equipment.

Motivation can stem from a sense of altruism, from momentum and peer pressure, or from clear incentives and opportunities for action. Disadvantaged smallholders teetering on survival are not likely to have clear incentives to support casual labourers more than they already do – which in itself is influenced by prevailing levels of trust and cultural norms, as well as individual personality. However, larger-scale smallholders may have more room for manoeuvre. Identifying potential benefits and incentives could also help to galvanize change: for example, fewer accidents during harvesting might be less disruptive for smallholder farmers and benefit the health of those working for them.

Increased demands for greater visibility of and transparency in the entire supply chain are being made of global companies. Many value chain actors share an interest in securing supply of agricultural produce and achieving greater sustainability in production in supply chains. For mission-driven traders and development actors there is a moral case for action. Yet the informal economy currently lacks visibility in development discourse and policy-making, despite its significant local and global economic value. The same could be said from a value chain and certification lens; the role of informal workers is neglected by Fairtrade and sustainability standards.

There are major barriers for sustainability standards to tackle this issue and expectations have to be realistic in terms of what a non-market mechanism can deliver. Such standards can already have exclusionary effects in some instances and heaping additional requirements on to standards could ultimately have unintended negative implications. In a sense, Fairtrade promotes a kind of formalization itself, with its offer of standards and auditing, as well as producer support. Finding a balance of the right kind of formalization, if this is needed at all, that is context specific is required. Fairtrade and other sustainability standards can make a contribution, but also need to avoid inappropriate policies and steps. There are already attempts to make sustainability standards more reachable (i.e. less costly and burdensome) for smallholder groups (ISEAL, 2011), as well as countless examples of public–private partnerships which leverage funding and capacity strengthening for smallholder production systems and could play a greater role in this regard. Sustainability standards and public–private partnerships should recognize the basic rights and livelihood strategies of informal economy workers in all their diversity. There are opportunities for standards, companies, and development organizations to shine a light on the position of casual workers and their terms of integration into value chains, including certified ones, and to take practical steps to increase their impact.

The limits to the effectiveness of sustainability standards in tackling systemic issues such as poverty and environmental unsustainability are becoming more widely understood (Nelson and Martin, 2013; Marx, 2016). Smallholders in Fairtrade are often on low incomes themselves, with low literacy levels and limited capacities and resources to implement improved decent working conditions. However, Fairtrade seeks to deliver fairer trading relationships in value chains and to address matters of social justice, so have particular responsibility to consider all chain actors who are disadvantaged. There are clear limits to what sustainability standards and Fairtrade can do, in part because of the very model they are based upon – standards and certification. At the same time Fairtrade, in particular, has other aspects to its theory of change; its work to strengthen producer organizations and networks is a case in point and a potential vehicle for recognizing not only smallholders, but also informal workers' rights and interests.

About the authors

Valerie Nelson is a reader in international development and a social scientist at the Natural Resources Institute, University of Greenwich. She leads the Equitable Trade and Responsible Business Programme at the NRI and has conducted consultancies and research on the impact of sustainability standards, codes, and initiatives in global value chains.

Dr David Phillips is a sustainable food supply and responsible sourcing expert, currently working as a Food & Drink Sector Specialist for WRAP (Waste and Resources Action Programme). Previously, he conducted extensive work in research and implementation of sustainable sourcing initiatives such as Fair Trade, including PhD research on hired labour in the sugar sector in Malawi.

Endnotes

1. These studies include: Poverty Impact of Voluntary Sustainability Standards funded by the UK Government Department for International Development (DFID), Early Impacts of the Adoption of the Better Cotton Initiative in Kurnool District, Andhra Pradesh (ISEAL funded), Fairtrade Coffee Impact Assessments.
2. Conducted by the NRI and commissioned by the UK Department for International Development (DFID) (2009–2013).
3. This study is being conducted by a consortium of partners led by the Natural Resources Institute (NRI) and including Pragmatix, Gujarat Institute of Development Research, and CESS. It is funded by ISEAL in collaboration with Better Cotton Initiative.

References

Barrientos, S., Gereffi, G. and Rossi, A. (2011) 'Economic and social upgrading in global production networks: a new paradigm for a changing world', *International Labour Review* 150(3–4): 319–40 <http://dx.doi.org/10.1111/j.1564-913X.2011.00119.x>.

Blowfield, M., Collinson, C., Chan, M.K., Nelson, V. and Maynard, B. (1999) 'Ethical trade and sustainable rural livelihoods', in D. Carney (ed.), *Sustainable Rural Livelihoods: What Contribution Can we Make?* London: DFID.

Bolwig, S., Ponte, S., du Toit, A., Riisgaard, L. and Halberg, N. (2008) *Integrating Poverty, Gender and Environmental Concerns into Value Chain Analysis: A Conceptual Framework and Lessons for Action Research* [pdf], DIIS Working Paper, 2008/16, Copenhagen: Danish Institute for International Studies <http://pure.diis.dk/ws/files/56383/WP08_16_Integrating_Poverty_Gender_and_Environmental_Concerns_into_Value_Chain_Analysis.pdf> [accessed 30 January 2017].

Byerlee, D. and Rueda, X. (2015) 'From public to private standards for tropical commodities: a century of global discourse on land governance on the forest frontier', *Forests* 6: 1301–24 <http://dx.doi.org/10.3390/f6041301>.

Cepeda, D., Pound, B., Nelson, V., Kajman, G., Cabascango, D., Martin, A., Chile, M., Posthumus, H., Caza, G., Mejia, I., Montenegro, F., Ruup, L., Velastegui, G.A., Tiaguaro, Y., Valverde, M. and Ojeda, A. (2013) *Assessing the Poverty Impact of Sustainability Standards: Ecuadorian Cocoa* [pdf], Chatham, UK: Natural Resources Institute <www.nri.org/images/documents/project_websites/AssessingPovertyImpacts/APISS-EcuadorianCocoa.pdf> [accessed 17 February 2017].

Chen, M.A. (2007) *Rethinking the Informal Economy: Linkages with Formal Economy and the Formal Regulatory Environment*, DESA Working paper No. 46, New York: UN Department of Economic and Social affairs.

Cramer, C., Johnston, D., Oya, C. and Sender, J. (2016) 'Fairtrade and labour markets in Ethiopia and Uganda', *Journal of Development Studies* 53: 841–56 <http://doi.org/10.1080/00220388.2016.1208175>.

Devey, R., Skinner, C. and Valodia, I. (2007) 'Definitions, data and the informal economy', in V. Padayachee (ed.), *The Development Decade: Economic and Social Change in South Africa, 1994–2004*, pp. 302–23, South Africa: Human Sciences Research Council.

Dolan, C. (2008) 'In the mists of development: fairtrade in Kenyan tea fields', *Globalizations* 5(2): 305–18 <http://dx.doi.org/10.1080/14747730802057787>.

Dolan, C. (2010) 'Virtual moralities: the mainstreaming of Fairtrade in Kenyan tea fields', *Geoforum* 41: 33–43.

Fairtrade International (FLO) (2011a) *Fairtrade Standard for Hired Labour* [pdf], Bonn, Germany: Fairtrade International <https://www.fairtrade.net/fileadmin/user_upload/content/2011-12-29-HL_EN.pdf> [accessed 6 March 2017].

FLO (2011b) *Fair Trade Glossary* [pdf], Bonn, Germany: Fairtrade International <https://www.fairtrade.net/fileadmin/user_upload/content/2009/about_fairtrade/2011-06-28_fair-trade-glossary_WFTO-FLO-FLOCERT.pdf> [accessed 6 March 2017].

FLO (2011c) Fairtrade Standard for Small Producer Organizations [pdf], Bonn, Germany: Fairtrade International <https://www.fairtrade.net/fileadmin/user_upload/content/2009/standards/documents/generic-standards/SPO_EN.pdf> [accessed 7 March 2017].

Fairtrade International (2015) *Fairtrade Theory of Change* [pdf] <www.fairtrade.net/fileadmin/user_upload/content/2009/resources/140112_Theory_of_Change_and_Indicators_Public.pdf> [accessed 7 March 2017].

FAO (2015) *2015–16 The State of Agricultural Commodity Markets. Trade and Food Security: Achieving a Better Balance between National Priorities and the Collective Good* [pdf], Rome: FAO <www.fao.org/3/a-i5090e.pdf> [accessed 7 March 2017].

Guha-Khasnobis, B., Kanbur, R. and Ostrom, E. (2007) *Linking the Formal and Informal Economy: Concepts and Policies*, WIDER Studies in Development Economics, Oxford: Oxford University Press.

Hart, K. (1973) 'Informal income opportunities and urban employment in Ghana', *Journal of Modern African Studies* 11(1): 61–89.

Hospes, O. (2014) 'Marking the success or end of global multi-stakeholder governance? The rise of national sustainability standards in Indonesia and Brazil for palm oil and soy', *Journal of Agriculture and Human Values* 31(3): 425–37 <http://dx.doi.org/10.1007/s10460-014-9511-9>.

ILO (2015) 'World Employment and Social Outlook 2015' [online], Geneva: ILO <www.ilo.org/global/about-the-ilo/multimedia/maps-and-charts/WCMS_369618/lang--en/index.htm?utm_content=bufferd25ee&utm_medium=social&utm_source=twitter.com&utm_campaign=buffer> [accessed 6 March 2017].

ISEAL (2011) *Stepwise Approaches as a Strategy for Scaling Up: Background report – April 2011* [pdf], London: ISEAL Alliance <www.isealalliance.org/sites/default/files/Stepwise_Approaches_Background_Report_April2011.pdf> [accessed 30 January 2017].

Kasente, D. (2012) 'Fair Trade and organic certification in value chains: lessons from a gender analysis from coffee exporting in Uganda', *Gender & Development* 20(1): 111–27 <http://dx.doi.org/10.1080/13552074.2012.663627>.

Kumar, R., Nelson, V., Martin, A., Badal, D., Latheef, A., Suresh Reddy, B., Narayanan, L., Young, S. and Hartog, M. (2015) *Evaluation of the Early Impacts of the Better Cotton Initiative on Smallholder Cotton Producers in Kurnool District, India: Baseline Report*, Natural Resources Institute, Centre for Economic and Social Studies, Gujarat Institute of Development Research, and Pragmatix for ISEAL Alliance and Better Cotton Initiative.

Lewis, S. (2016) *Informality and Inclusive Green Growth: Evidence from the 'Biggest Private Sector' Event* [pdf], 25 February 2016, London: International Institute for Environment and Development (IIED) <http://pubs.iied.org/pdfs/17365IIED.pdf> [accessed 15 January 2017].

Makita, R. (2012) 'Fair trade certification: the case of tea plantation workers in India', Development Policy Review 30(1): 87–107 <http://dx.doi.org/10.11 11/j.1467-7679.2012.00561.x>.

Mallet, P. (2016) *How Sustainability Standards can Contribute to Landscape Approaches and Zero Deforestation Commitments,* London: ISEAL Alliance.

Marx, A. (2016) 'Legitimacy, institutional design, and dispute settlement: the case of eco-certification systems', *Globalizations* 11(3): 401–16.

Neilson, N. and Pritchard, B. (2010) 'Fairness and ethicality in their place: the regional dynamics of fair trade and ethical sourcing agendas in the plantation districts of South India' , *Environment and Planning* 42(8): 1833–51 <https://doi.org/10.1068/a4260> .

Nelson, V. and Martin, A. (2012) 'The impact of fairtrade: evidence, shaping factors, and future pathways', *Food Chain* 2(1): 42–63 <http://dx.doi. org/10.3362/2046-1887.2012.005>.

Nelson, V. and Martin, A. (2013) *Final Technical Report: Assessing the Poverty Impact of Voluntary Sustainability Standards* [pdf], Chatham, UK: NRI report for DFID.

Nelson, V. and Martin, A. (2014) 'Fairtrade International's multi-dimensional impacts in Africa', in L. Raynolds and E. Bennett (eds), *Handbook of Research on Fair Trade*, pp. 509–31, Cheltenham, UK: Edward Elgar Publishing.

Nelson, V. and Pound, B. (2009) *The Last Ten Years: A Comprehensive Review of the Literature on the Impact of Fairtrade* [pdf], Chatham, UK: Natural Resources Institute, University of Greenwich <https://www.fairtrade.net/fileadmin/user_upload/content/2009/about_us/2010_03_NRI_Full_Literature_Review.pdf> [accessed 21 February 2017].

Nelson, V. and Smith, S. (2011) *Fairtrade Cotton: Assessing impact in Mali, Senegal, Cameroon and India* [pdf], Chatham, UK: NRI Report for Fairtrade International.

Nelson, V. and Tallontire, A. (2014) 'Battlefields of ideas: changing narratives and power dynamics in private standards in global agricultural value chains', *Journal of Agriculture and Human Values* 31(3): 481–97 <http://dx.doi.org/10.1007/s10460-014-9512-8>.

Nelson, V., Galvez, M. and Blowfield, M. (2000) *Social Impact of Ethical and Conventional Brazil Nut Trading on Forest-Dependent People in Peru* [pdf], Chatham, UK: NRI <http://gala.gre.ac.uk/11838/1/11838_Nelson_Social%20impact%20of%20ethical%20%28monograph%29%202000.pdf> [accessed 7 March 2017].

Nelson, V., Tallontire, A. and Collinson, C. (2002) 'Assessing the potential of ethical trade schemes for forest dependent people: comparative experiences from Peru and Ecuador', *International Forestry Review* 4: 99–110.

Nelson, V., Opoku, K., Martin, A., Bugri, J. and Posthumus, H. (2013) *Final Report: Assessing the Poverty Impact of Sustainability Standards: Fairtrade in Ghanaian Cocoa* [pdf], Chatham, UK: NRI <www.nri.org/images/documents/project_websites/AssessingPovertyImpacts/APISS-FairtradeInGhanaian Cocoa.pdf> [accessed 7 March 2017].

Nelson, V., Tallontire, A. and Opondo, M. (2014) 'Pathways of transformation or transgression? Power relations, ethical space and labour rights', in *Food Transgressions: Making Sense of Contemporary Food Politics*, Ashgate Critical Food Studies, pp. 15–38, Abingdon, UK: Routledge.

Nelson, V., Haggar, J., Martin, A., Donovan, J., Borasino, E., Hasyim, W., Mhando, N., Senga, M., Mgumia, J., Quintanar Guadarrama, E., Kendar, Z., Valdez, J. and Morales, D. (2016) *Fairtrade Coffee: A Study to Assess the Impact of Fairtrade for Coffee Smallholders and Producer Organisations in Indonesia, Mexico, Peru, and Tanzania* [pdf], NRI and ICRAF report <https://www.fairtrade.net/fileadmin/user_upload/content/2009/resources/1611_NRI_Coffee_Evaluation-final_report.pdf> [accessed 7 March 2017].

Phillips, D. (2014) 'Uneven and unequal people-centered development: the case of Fair Trade and Malawi sugar producers', *Agriculture and Human Values* 31: 563–76 <http://dx.doi.org/10.1007/s10460-014-9500-z>.

Potts, J., Lynch, M., Wilkings, A., Huppe, G.A., Cunningham, M. and Voora, V. (2014) *State of Sustainability Initiatives Review 2014: Standards and the Green Economy* [pdf], Manitoba, Canada: IISD and London: IIED <www.iisd.org/sites/default/files/pdf/2014/ssi_2014.pdf> [accessed 21 February 2017].

Raynolds, L.T. (2012) 'Fair trade flowers: global certification, environmental sustainability, and labor standards', *Rural Sociology* 77(4): 493–519 <http://dx.doi.org/10.llll/j.l54W)831.2012.00090.x>.

Raynolds, L.T. (2014) 'Fairtrade, certification, and labor: global and local tensions in improving conditions for agricultural workers', *Agriculture and Human Values* 31: 499–511.

Raynolds, L.T., Murray, D. and Wilkinson, J. (2007) *Fair Trade*, London and New York: Routledge.

Renard, M.-C. (2003) 'Fair trade: quality, market and conventions', *Journal of Rural Studies* 19(1): 87–96.

Riisgaard, L. (2015) 'Fairtrade certification, conventions, and labor', in L.T. Raynolds and E.A. Bennett (eds), *Handbook of Research on Fair Trade*, pp. 120–38, Cheltenham, UK: Edward Elgar Publishing.

Riisgard, L. and Gibbon, P. (2014) 'Labour management on contemporary Kenyan cut flower farms: foundations of an industrial–civic compromise', *Journal of Agrarian Change* 14(2): 260–85 <http://dx.doi.org/10.1111/joac.12064>.

Riisgaard, L. and Hammer, N. (2014) 'Prospects for labour in global value chains: labour standards in the cut flower and banana industries', *British Journal of Industrial Relations* 49(1): 168–90.

Riisgaard, L., Bolwig, S., Ponte, S., Du Toit, A., Halberg, N. and Matose, F. (2010) 'Integrating poverty and environmental concerns into value-chain analysis: a strategic framework and practical guide', *Development Policy Review* 28(2): 195–216 <http://dx.doi.org/10.1111/j.1467-7679.2010.00481.x>.

Sikor, T., Auld, G., Bebbington, A.J., Benjaminsen, T.A., Gentry, B.S., Hunsberger, C., Izac, A.-M., Margulis, M., Plieninger, T., Schroeder, H., and Upton, C. (2013) 'Global land governance: from territory to flow?' *Current Opinion in Environmental Sustainability* 5(5): 522–7 <http://dx.doi.org/10.1016/j.cosust.2013.06.006>.

Smith, S. (2014) 'Fair trade and women's empowerment', in L.T. Raynolds and E.A. Bennett (eds), *Handbook of Research on Fair Trade*, Cheltenham, UK: Edward Elgar.

Standing, G. (2016) The Corruption of Capitalism: Why Rentiers Thrive and Work Does not Pay, London: Biteback Publishing Ltd.

Stathers, T. and Gathuthi, C. with Nelson, V., Martin, A., Posthumus, H., Kleih, U., Kamau, E., Gichohi, A., Kokonya, M., Umidha, N., Irimu, V. and Muhoro, A. (2013) *Final Report: Poverty Impact of Social and Environmental Voluntary Standard Systems in Kenyan Tea* [pdf], Chatham, UK: NRI <www.nri.org/images/documents/project_websites/AssessingPovertyImpacts/APISS-KenyanTea.pdf> [accessed 7 March 2017].

Stevis, D. (2015) 'Global labor politics and fair trade', in L.T. Raynolds and E.A. Bennett (eds), *Handbook of Research on Fair Trade*, pp. 102–19, Cheltenham, UK: Edward Elgar Publishing.

Tallontire, A. (2014) 'Fair trade and development in African agriculture' in L.T. Raynolds and E.A. Bennett (eds), *Handbook of Research on Fair Trade*, Cheltenham, UK: Edward Elgar Publishing.

Tallontire, A., Opondo, M., Nelson, V. and Martin, A. (2011) 'Beyond the vertical? Using value chains and governance as a framework to analyse private standards initiatives in agri-food chains', *Journal of Agriculture and Human Values* 28(3): 427–41 <http://dx.doi.org/10.1007/s10460-009-9237-2>.

Valkila, J. and Nygren, A. (2010) 'Impacts of Fair Trade certification on coffee farmers, cooperatives, and laborers in Nicaragua', *Agriculture and Human Values* 27: 321–33 <http://dx.doi.org/10.1007/ s10460-009-9208-7>.

Vorley, B., Cotula, L. and Chan, M.K. (2012) *Tipping the Balance: Policies to Shape Agricultural Investments and Markets in Favour of Small-scale Farmers*, Oxford, UK: IIED/Oxfam.

CHAPTER 8

Fairtrade, fair-trade, fair trade and ethical trade: reflections of a practitioner

Adam Brett

Abstract

This chapter aims to distinguish between the muddled terms of 'fairtrade', 'fair-trade' and 'fair trade', explained by an insider. The origins of the concept are explored, journeying from the 1970's to the present day. The chapter examines the most commonly asked questions about fair trade, including what exactly it is, why commodity prices rise and fall and what the impacts of it are, ultimately concluding that to participate in fair trade is to participate in a long-term, lasting strategy.

Keywords: Fairtrade, fair-trade, fair trade, ethical trade, commodities, FLO, child labour, long-term

Fairtrade (with a capital letter, and written as one word) is a trademark. It is illegal to use it on food products in Europe unless the product has been certified as being produced to Fairtrade standards by the European Fairtrade Labelling Initiative (FLO). Fair-trade (two words, with a hyphen) can be used by anyone, and means more or less the same as Fairtrade, but without the legality. All other variants (fair trade, ethical trade and so on) are used by different groups with different meanings in different contexts.

The purpose of this chapter is to cast some relatively lighthearted light on this muddled situation from the perspective of a long-term insider, hopefully informing and entertaining in equal measure. In the chapter the non-dogmatic form 'fair trade' is used to describe all fair trade activities. Where I am referring specifically to FLO Fairtrade products that legal form will be used.

Fair trade grew out of different social and political movements in different parts of Europe during the 1970s. At its inception, fair trade was a highly idealistic concept, usually based on the idea that markets were inherently unfair and exploitative, and that co-operative partnerships between producers in Southern countries linked to enlightened consumers in the North could overcome this exploitation and generate benefits for producers and consumers alike.

Those who initiated fair trade back then did so from widely diverging starting points: church community members, members of the European co-operative movements, people involved in political campaigns such as

http://dx.doi.org/10.3362/9781780449067.008

Nicaragua Solidarity, and a wide range of grass-roots organizations. Each group came to the process with its own idea of what fair trade was or should be. A small-scale factionalism, which is typical of many marginal oppositional political movements, developed along the lines of 'my version of fair trade is better than yours'. Many long hours were spent in meetings of differing groups of activists arguing out the points, with some unwilling to sell the products of the others.

Those involved in the movement started from a belief that conventional capitalist mechanisms of trade were inefficient, and that a coming socialist revolution would sweep all this away and replace it with a world of fairness, milk and honey. These people thought of fair trade as the starting point for a broader and deeper revolution in society. Through the 1990s this idealism gradually gave way as it came into contact with reality. Those in the Fairtrade movement who were actually buying and trading with Southern partner businesses came to realize that while there were many faults in conventional capitalist mechanisms of trade, none of these faults was easily overturned, and usually the processes which seemed exploitative and unfair on the surface resulted from far deeper structural realities of the wider world of trade. The hard-knocks of trading in the marketplace were a powerful training ground for fair trade pioneers, and one tribute to the movement is the longevity and stamina of many of those who have involved themselves in it. We took our knocks, learned and grew.

What we refer to today as fair trade would be virtually unrecognisable to the early pioneers. The idea of a FLO Fairtrade marked 'Kit Kat' (a chocolate confectionery product), or a market for Fairtrade products worth close to £1 bn worldwide would I believe be almost unimaginable. Fairtrade tea, coffee and chocolate are now such well-established concepts that some larger retailers only sell FLO Fairtrade versions of the products. Of course the journey from the 1970s to the present has been one of development, adaptation and compromise.

The commodities see-saw: Why do commodity prices swing?

The starting point for many fair trade campaigns in the 1970s was the horrific suffering of South American and African farmers in the face of severe reductions in the purchasing power of their cash crops, such as coffee and cocoa. Commodity prices fell in nominal and real terms for year after year, reducing to penury many farmers with long-term commitments to a particular cash crop. These were crops that took many years to establish; farmers could not easily switch in and out of production; so they were basically trapped with their net income each year in the hands of the market. This process was seen as completely unfair. Prices for finished products such as retail packs of instant coffee were stable or rose, but the price received by farmers fell. What was happening in the middle? From the perspective of the less than perfectly informed fair trade activist, the giant multinationals were taking super profits and exploiting the poor, small Southern farmer. Of course the reality was more complex than this, but it was definitely true to say that from the 1950s or 1970s through to the early 2000s, global commodity prices in general fell in value to the detriment of the producer countries.

World demand for commodities is enormously complex, with products rising and falling in favour with customer groups and the interplay of consumers' purchasing power in different countries. As an example, at present there is an unprecedented rise in the cost of cocoa which some claim is due to rising demand for chocolate products by the previously non-chocolate consuming Chinese. The world commodity price instability is a direct consequence of the fact that global supply/production of each key commodity also varies exogenously. A frost in Brazil or a bacterial wilt in East Africa is not guaranteed to coincide with a reduction in global demand; in fact demand may rise at the precise moment when supply is at its weakest.

The situation is probably made more, rather than less, complex by the large-scale action of agencies such as the World Bank. Interventions such as substantial investments in coffee production in Vietnam occur while other producer countries continue or expand their own production. Suddenly the world market sees production levels that exceed immediate demand. Commodity products have a limited shelf life and traders have to sell or face a 100 per cent loss if the product spoils, so products are sold at prices below the cost of production.

Many supply chains are long, and contain extensive opportunities for speculation, which further destabilizes prices. Cotton is a key example of this, where the commodity is traded as seed, fibre, yarn and cloth before finally being transformed into garments for sale to the consumer. Spot markets for the commodity at each step in this chain see speculatively driven price swings that are often out of synchronization with each other, adding greatly to the risk for those involved in the industries.

What (or who) is fair trade?

One of the central tenets of fair trade (in all its flavours) from the outset, was a 'normalization' or reduction in price fluctuation and speculation. Fair trade tends to operate by setting a minimum price that is linked to the cost of production. If the world price rises above this minimum price then the farmer may receive more, but if the world price falls below the minimum price the fair trade buyer must continue to pay the minimum price. In addition to this minimum price, the fair trade farmer should also receive a 'social premium' which is an extra payment to the farmer, plus other forms of less direct assistance, such as help with the local development and management of the farmers' supply chain, guaranteed forward planning and forward ordering.

In some commodities there is also a 'fair trade maximum price'. The idea is that if the Northern buyer is being generous during the price down-swing by continuing to pay the fair trade minimum, surely the same buyer should get something back during the times of peak prices. In practice this 'maximum' is rarely acted upon, primarily because small-scale farmers rarely have the maturity or long-term vision to remain loyal to their fair trade buyer during the good times. If they can sell for more they do, leaving the fair trade buyer with nothing. Given this, in practice the fair trade buyer tends to pay the full market price during the peak periods, but pay at least the fair trade minimum price the rest of the time.

Conventional economists tend to react with horror to the idea of fixing prices, as they believe that this is always wrong and is guaranteed to result in over production or inefficient allocation of resources. A key point for those wishing to counter this argument is that the fair trade minimum price is set at a level that delivers no profit to the farmer. It is intended as a mechanism to assist the survival of the farmer during periods of excessive world price fluctuation. Given the cost of re-establishing a farm producing a crop such as coffee, there is a simple economic rationale in a process that damps the level of price variability in the market. Otherwise farmers waste valuable resources, expending energy destroying and re-establishing fields of crops as the world price see-saws violently up and down over time. Also, as with mechanisms such as unemployment benefit or welfare payments, there is a purely social argument for such minimum prices as they guarantee human dignity and reduce suffering. Beyond the minimum price and the idea that fair trade should work on the basis of long-term partnerships between buyers in the North and producers in the South, there is not terribly much agreement on what really constitutes fair trade.

FLO, the main European voice for fair trade, has very clear standards for what it says fair trade is. In the USA a similar role is taken by Transfair. The FLO Fairtrade symbol is the most widely recognized consumer logo representing fair trade and we are reaching a stage where people are starting to say that FLO Fairtrade (with a capital 'F' and spelt as one word) is the primary or only definition of fair trade, but this is definitely a simplification. The people working at the World Fair Trade Organization (formerly IFAT) and at labelling organizations such as Rainforest Alliance definitely believe that there is more to fair trade than FLO Fairtrade. A number of small businesses conduct fair trade without engaging with FLO, seeing it as a cumbersome bureaucracy. These small businesses have to communicate the fair trade message of their product without relying on the advertising and public relations skills, or the substantial public, international aid agency and donor support which FLO commands.

FLO Fairtrade is without doubt the dominant force in fair trade: many retailers only recognize the FLO symbol and do not carry alternative symbols. In any case, the FLO symbol is overridingly dominant in the marketplace.

This said, it is now also true to say that the European marketplace for most commodities is characterized by a complex range of different auditing and marking systems; FLO Fairtrade is only a small part of a larger jigsaw puzzle, which includes auditing standards such as Organic, GlobalGAP, RSPO (for palm oil), FSC (for wood products) and many others. We live in the era of the audit, standard or certification process.

FLO Fairtrade involves a minimum price, long-term buying relationships, and a social premium for the farmers involved in the production of the raw materials in the South. Beyond these primary tenets, meeting the fair trade standard involves a number of other detailed issues that are outlined in certification standards. Producers wishing to carry the FLO mark must submit themselves to independent auditing by an external certifying officer to verify that they meet these standards: a process that carries a very significant cost. FLO charges a fee for all businesses that retail products with their mark, and also charges a fee for all farmer groups that submit to certification. Those involved also carry additional production costs, compared with non-fair trade producers, in a number of ways. For example, their employees are required to be paid at levels which often exceed local wage norms, and there are a range of requirements on issues such as child labour, which may raise the cost of FLO Fairtrade products compared with products produced on the open market.

All of these factors combine with the basic fact that most fair trade still operates between relatively small businesses (and therefore is relatively low-volume and does not achieve economies of scale) to produce a situation where fair trade and Fairtrade products are often significantly more expensive than conventional market equivalents. Some supermarkets exacerbate the problem by demanding that Fairtrade products deliver higher profit margins than conventional products, pushing the price to the consumer higher still. The price difference between the fair trade and conventional version of a product is much larger than the difference in price paid to the farmer, leading consumers to complain that they are being 'ripped off'.

Sometimes it feels as though we are back in the 1970s again, but now it is the fair trade business people themselves who are being accused of exploitation and corruption. Of course fair trade business people are not corrupt: they simply operate in the context of these multiple disadvantages while trying to do the best they can. A typical example of this is a when a conventional product receives support from a retailer. A big supermarket might decide to run a publicity campaign with a multi-million dollar, euro or pound budget. Part of this budget could be given to offering a low price to the consumer. The supermarket sells the product at a loss, but gains publicity and 'footfall' (number of customers entering the store). These irrationally priced products – and there are many hundreds of them in every supermarket – confuse the consumer, who assumes they reflect the products' true cost of production. The consumer compares prices on these products with the prices he or she pays for fair trade products and again feels ripped off. But the problem is not caused by exploitative pricing by fair trade business people; rather it is a function of the irrational pricing policies of the supermarkets.

What are the real impacts of fair trade?

The fair trade mantra of minimum price, long-term relationship and social premium is trotted out whenever this question is posed, but I for one doubt that these represent the most significant aspects of the trade. Returning to the issue of child labour, which interestingly is one of the areas where fair trade can have its strongest social impacts via indirect as well as direct influence, let us start with an admission: child labour is relatively endemic in cocoa production in West Africa. Children work on their parents' farms as a matter of course, which is really not laudable, but at least parents are generally careful in regard to the range of work their children do and try their best to send their children to school where one is available. But there is also extensive trafficking of children around the West African region to work on farms in terrible conditions on the fringes of the trade.

FLO Fairtrade has made a strong stand on this: FLO standards specifically exclude child labour and evidence of it is justification for immediate exclusion from FLO certification. FLO has done excellent work moving children from cocoa fields into schools, and in direct training to farmers and cocoacollection company staff on this issue. FLO's stand has forced many of the larger players in the cocoa sector to wake up and pay attention. Child labour is now high on the agenda right across the cocoa producing industry in the Fairtrade, fair trade, ethical and conventional sectors. There are a number of other examples where fair trade business practices are increasingly coming to be the norm in conventional business. Organic labelling can claim similar victories in their own sector of sustainable farming practices: cases where particularly damaging chemicals have now been removed from the conventional trade, or where less destructive farming practices are now recognized and used by conventional farmers. Advocates of GlobalGAP make similar claims for the beneficial 'catalytic' impact of their work.

Larger firms do not want to be perceived as bad guys: their brands have value that is rapidly eroded if they are tarnished by association with inhumane or environmentally damaging practices. At the same time the world of European campaigning is fickle and more fashiondriven than it is willing to accept. Hardened campaigners may stick to their chosen political topic for years, but the general public bores easily and quickly moves on to the next big issue. Hard-won gains from Fairtrade campaigners can be eroded surprisingly quickly if the public looks away and bigger business interests apply their substantial market power to breaking down the carefully constructed fair trade systems.

The key point is that measuring the impact of fair trade is hard. Speaking personally, I cannot see how any assessment methodology could incorporate a measure for the fact that conventional trade has been forced to improve as a result of the pressure from fair trade. The methodologies mostly involve simple like-for-like comparisons between the social conditions of farmers involved in fair trade and those involved in conventional trade. They rarely even involve any significant long-term analysis, which might uncover the greater security of income experienced by fair trade farmers, let alone try to measure the catalytic impact of fair trade on the wider economy or conventional trade systems. There is clear evidence that fair trade has raised the bar for practice in the conventional sector, but quantifying this is virtually impossible.

The development 'industry' now seems to have ethical trade, fair trade, fair-trade and Fairtrade firmly in its sights. Having ticked along for years ignoring the marketplace altogether, development agencies have woken up to the fact that there is no point in training farmers to grow more of their product if they are unable to sell it. A slew of big-word policies such as 'making markets work for the poor' have been announced and agencies have identified some variant of ethical or fair trade as a possible route to achieving these goals. Hardly a day goes by without one study group or another getting in touch with me to explain that they have received funding to run a sectoral analysis, value chain review or baseline survey to assess the impact of fair trade in East, West or Southern Africa. They then announce their methodologies and workplans, and most frighteningly of all, state that some major agency or other will decide whether or not to spend a significant amount of money on 'fair trade' based on the results of their research.

The sudden donor agency interest in fair trade seems likely to be as ephemeral as any number of other big ideas that have come and gone in the development sector over the last decade. There is little doubt that in two or three years time the development agenda will have moved on to pastures new, with agency experts nodding to each other as they agree with each other that fair trade was a wasted effort which never really delivered any measurable benefits. The reality of course is that it is impossible for fair trade, or Fairtrade to be adopted casually as a policy or strategy. Those who do so are almost bound to fail, and those measuring these flawed versions of fair trade will see little or no benefit accruing to farmers or other Southern participants.

Fair trade starts first as a contract between equals who agree to trade together for the long-term; a form of partnership that is almost like marriage. I am still trading with people I first met more than 20 years ago and will probably continue to do so for as long as my business exists. Through those 20 years we have learned and suffered together, informed each other and co-operated. We now know and trust each other and collaborate well; we understand each other in ways that only those who have such depth of mutual experience can. When I travel to meet these partners I meet the children of the people who started to work with me all that time ago. The children are educated, often very well, and have grown up in environments with a reasonable amount of stability and security. They and the stability that their households experience are the real measurable outputs from the trade we began all those years ago. The educated children and the stability that their households experience are the real measurable outputs from our trade.

Conventional business people regularly contact me to find out how they can 'invest in' fair trade. What they actually want to know is how they can make a quick profit out of it. The process is always the same: the first phone call explains that they have money to invest and they want to 'make a difference'. Then comes a meeting at which they talk about the bucket-loads of cash they have, and how they are willing to put millions into the right kind of venture. At this stage there is usually still a pretence of philanthropy. Beyond this, things vary a bit from case to case, but the end is always the same: they ask how much we need to build the business up so that it can be sold on for a quick buck and a massive return; 'achieving exit' is a typical dubious euphemism. When I explain that there is no exit with fair trade, it is for the long-term, it is about relationships, learning about people and building something lasting, they look at me as though I am insane. From time to time I have thought they were right, but last year I met Muhammad Yunus (a Bangladeshi economist and founder of the Grameen Bank) and, having talked to him, I know that I am not.

About the author

Adam Brett is the founder director of fair trade pioneer business, Tropical Wholefoods, founded in 1990. The opinions expressed in this chapter are entirely his own, and are not intended to represent the opinions of the Fairtrade, fair-trade or fair trade movement.

CHAPTER 9

Debate: 'Does Fairtrade have more impact than conventional trade or trade certified by other sustainability standards?'

Matthew Anderson, Philip Booth and Sushil Mohan

Abstract

Matthew Anderson, Philip Booth and Sushil Mohan, three respected professionals with insider knowledge of the Fairtrade market, discuss the impact of Fairtrade compared with other sustainability certified and conventional trade.

Dear Sushil and Philip,

As the Fairtrade Foundation prepares to celebrate the 20th anniversary of the Fairtrade Mark in the UK, it seems like an opportune moment to reflect on the impact of Fairtrade and how its approach to trade and development contrasts with other sustainability standards and the practices of conventional trade.

Fairtrade is an alternative approach to conventional trade and the most widely recognized ethical label globally. It is a strategy for poverty alleviation and sustainable development through ensuring the payment of a minimum price and of a defined additional (development) premium. Its purpose is to create opportunities for small-scale farmers and workers who have been economically disadvantaged or marginalized by the conventional trading system.

Over 70 per cent of the British public now recognize the Fairtrade Mark, and nine in 10 consumers who recognize the Fairtrade Mark regard it as a trusted label (GlobeScan, 2011). This awareness has translated into retail sales of over £1.5 bn in 2012 and there are signs that Fairtrade is moving from the margins to mainstream. One in every three bananas sold in the UK, and 44 per cent of bagged sugar, is now Fairtrade certified. These sales contribute to the £23.3 m Fairtrade premium that is returned to producer organizations annually from sales of Fairtrade labelled products to consumers in the UK.

The academic body of literature exploring the impact of Fairtrade has developed substantially over the last decade and while it can be difficult to attribute economic and social impact from individual studies, a systematic analysis of the existing evidence base reveals a number of areas where Fairtrade supports positive organizational and community development (Nelson and Pound,

http://dx.doi.org/10.3362/9781780449067.009

2009). The economic benefits of Fairtrade are evidenced in the higher returns and stable incomes reported in a high proportion of these impact studies. However, even in situations where household income has not improved, many studies suggest that Fairtrade still offers a range of benefits such as: increased access to credit, increased self-esteem, benefits for the wider community, and organizational capacity building (Nelson and Pound, 2009).

Although harder to quantify, the published literature also strongly supports the argument that Fairtrade is having positive empowerment impacts (Nelson and Pound, 2009). The positive impacts on producer empowerment have been identified in two dimensions: 1) *empowerment for individual producers* – improved producer self-confidence, improved market and export knowledge, greater access to training; and 2) *organizational strengthening* – increased influence nationally and locally, improved democracy in decision-making and levels of participation, stronger organizations able to survive in hard times, and higher ability to attract other sources of funding.

A direct comparison between Fairtrade and conventional trade presents a number of methodological challenges, particularly since non-Fairtrade operations often refuse to participate in studies – citing cost implications and resource constraints. While these commercial considerations may be understandable, the limited transparency in conventional supply chains serves to undermine consumer trust, and reinforces the need for third-party certification.

Similarly, there are few direct comparisons with other sustainability standards – although survey tools, such as those being pioneered by the Committee on Sustainability Assessment (COSA), may make the application of comparative research methods more feasible in the future. Current studies suggest that on ecological and environmental criteria, UTZ Certified and Rainforest Alliance demonstrate a more specific and tangible impact on key sustainability indicators. Despite these limitations, Fairtrade remains a unique tool to promote development and empowerment among marginalized rural communities in the Global South.

Best wishes,
Matthew

Dear Matthew,
Fairtrade is part of the rich tapestry of institutions that develops in market economies to bring together consumers and producers. Fairtrade opens up an additional trading channel within the market in a way that matches consumer preferences to the needs of many producers.

However, it does not alter the market fundamentals. The demand and supply conditions for Fairtrade products follow conventional trade practices. Upstream actors in the supply chain exert economic and quality control taking account of consumers' preferences. Fairtrade growth, like conventional trade, is fuelled by the increasing involvement of mainstream corporate and retail circuits.

It is therefore simplistic to assert that Fairtrade corrects inequitable trade because Fairtrade is not changing the market basics. Furthermore,

Fairtrade is not for the poor and marginal producer as it is difficult for them to meet the Fairtrade requirements. The beneficiaries of Fairtrade activity, by and large, are not the world's poorest people.

Of course, like other speciality market producers, Fairtrade producers benefit from the additional trade channel that is opened up. But so do a very large number of conventional market producers – and other labelling schemes such as Rainforest Alliance. Most conventional trade buyers want stable supply chains and good relationships with suppliers and Fairtrade is not unique in achieving such relationships. For example, the growth of speciality coffee, encouraged by buyers, provides a huge premium for growers and has led to much greater prosperity in Africa's poorest countries.

Despite the growing visibility of Fairtrade in some Western markets and some products, one cannot ignore the fact that Fairtrade sales represent only around 0.01 per cent of the total food and beverage industry sales worldwide (Mohan, 2010). So, when it comes to the relief of poverty, Fairtrade will always be a bit-part player.

The main drivers of poverty reduction are peace and stability, the rule of law, the protection of property rights, good systems of justice, and the right conditions for enterprise and markets to work. This includes a commitment to free trade.

Fairtrade is a small player in a general environment of institutional and policy improvements in many poor countries. It is these other policy improvements that lead to greater competition for labour, more efficient supply chains, and the movement into higher-value-added production that are the sustainable solution to poverty.

It is not Fairtrade that has in recent years led to the highest level of economic growth in sub-Saharan Africa in its history; it is not Fairtrade that has led to significant reductions in inequality in Africa. It is the extension of free trade that has lifted hundreds of millions out of absolute poverty in countries such as Vietnam, China, and India. Indeed, those poor economies that opened to trade grew three times faster in the 1990s than those that did not (OECD, n.d.).

Thankfully the Fairtrade Foundation has fallen relatively silent on the issue, but it was certainly not helpful in the 1990s and early 2000s when it was making the case for more trade regulation – a policy destined to promote bad governance and increase poverty. There is enormous potential for much greater poverty reductions in India, Pakistan, and Bangladesh but, again, Fairtrade is largely irrelevant. Of course, significant responsibility lies with developed economies too. They should reduce their trade barriers (for example in cotton, sugar, and rice). This would also help the poor, but not because of Fairtrade.

To repeat, we welcome Fairtrade! We believe in a market economy. We approve of private certification schemes (though the cost of such schemes should be borne in mind and those promoting such schemes should not use soft or hard coercion to promote membership).

Fairtrade deserves credit for opening up a trade channel that provides an additional marketing opportunity for some producers and possibly allowing them to capture a price premium. That participation brings greater diversification, empowerment, and capacity building.

However, Fairtrade is to the primary product market what the fan-owned clubs such as Exeter City and Wycombe Wanderers are to the football league in England and Wales – welcome institutional diversity, but not of huge significance.

Best wishes,
Philip and Sushil

Dear Philip and Sushil,
Thank you for your response. There is much that I agree with in your account of the development benefits of conventional trade and enterprise. However, the reality is that almost 1.3 billion people still live below the global poverty line (Chen and Ravallion, 2008: 44). Unfortunately many of the benefits of economic growth are not trickling down quick enough, if at all.

Smallholder farmers are among those that often find themselves economically marginalized and trapped in a cycle of poverty. There is evidence from recent studies that half of the world's hungriest people are themselves smallholder farmers (IAASTD, 2008). Despite being part of potentially lucrative international supply chains, smallholders producing commodity cash crops remain disempowered within them. Commodity production and trade are dominated by large transnational corporations (TNCs) resulting in low returns to growers. Even when world commodity prices are high, it is the

large TNCs and financial investors that tend to capture most of the gains (UNCTAD, 2012: 13).

While still a small proportion of total global trade, the institutional diversity that Fairtrade offers presents an opportunity for mainstream businesses to engage in trading partnerships that genuinely benefit those within their global supply chains. And as Fairtrade develops and expands, so does its geographic diversity. Figures from 2011 show that 59 per cent of all farmers and workers within the Fairtrade system live in Africa, with Kenya having the highest number of people participating in Fairtrade overall (Fairtrade International, 2012: 18).

Understandably it takes time to alter the market fundamentals, but there is evidence that this is happening. As businesses look for alternative models that are able to deliver mutually beneficial sustainable supply chains, Fairtrade is acting as a moral entrepreneur – disrupting old institutions and initiating new ones. Perhaps one of the clearest examples of this is in the banana supply chain, and the conversion of UK supermarket chain Sainsbury's to 100% Fairtrade bananas.

In 2006, Sainsbury's initiated a review of its entire banana supply base. Matt North, Sainsbury's banana and citrus fruit buyer at the time, began to ask questions about living standards and what could be done to improve the situation for grower communities. North decided that although the Rainforest Alliance mark would have been easier to achieve, no real social benefits were returned to the communities (North, 2011: 145). The only way to achieve a real difference was through Fairtrade and the only way to achieve this with real scale was by converting the entire range of bananas to Fairtrade (North, 2011: 146). Interestingly the driver for this supply chain overhaul was only partly a response to consumer preference. One in five customers were already choosing to purchase Fairtrade bananas, but Sainsbury's were still not able to sell all of the Fairtrade bananas available from the growers (North, 2011: 140).

Sainsbury's now sells 650 million Fairtrade bananas each year and in addition to the guaranteed minimum price for their crop, the Fairtrade banana partnership generates around £4 m annually in Fairtrade premiums. This conversion to Fairtrade represented a significant investment (equivalent to 2 per cent of Sainsbury's operating profit). It also involved supporting suppliers through the certification process and Fyffes' rescheduling of shipping arrangements to provide a direct service from Colombia to Portsmouth on a weekly basis (North, 2011: 150). But the significance of this conversion went beyond Sainsbury's own supply chain. When Waitrose and Co-op announced that they would also convert all of their bananas to Fairtrade, Matt North's work became a catalyst for change.

Building scale remains a challenge for Fairtrade; but with the growing support of a range of retailers and major brands, producers will continue to benefit from increasing volumes of Fairtrade sales and profit from their involvement in sustainable trading partnerships.

Best wishes,
Matthew

Dear Matthew,
While we agree with much that you have written and repeat that we see Fairtrade as a welcome part of the market economy – and certainly not separate from it – there are perhaps two main differences between us. The first relates to the scale of Fairtrade: How much difference does it really make? The second is the ability of the extension of trade, globalization, and good governance to make many more people better off more quickly than Fairtrade can (though, of course, we do not see the two as mutually exclusive).

However, another issue has arisen which is important too. You say: 'There is evidence from recent studies that half of the world's hungriest people [say, 650 million] are themselves smallholder farmers'. We agree, but Fairtrade is not going to dramatically change this. Free trade may raise global prices for certain products where there is currently Western protectionism and Fairtrade might provide them with slightly higher prices. However, given that there are currently only 7.5 million Fairtrade workers (including their families and those who are not farmers) (Traidcraft, 2014), Fairtrade is too small to contribute significantly to resolve this problem. Furthermore, the bulk of Fairtrade workers are not smallholders partly because of the certification requirements (Mohan, 2010).

As the discussion of bananas above shows, Fairtrade might be able to raise the living standards of growers by about 5 per cent if all the premium was used for the benefit of the growers. In addition, Fairtrade might provide some price stability when market conditions fluctuate. But even this is doubtful. A Fairtrade contract involves fixing prices for the producer so that a guaranteed price, higher than conventional world market price, is received regardless of supply and demand conditions at the time the product is delivered. A literal interpretation of this contract condition has resulted in the propagation of a fallacy, which finds expression in the view that Fairtrade protects primary product producers against the volatility of market prices. However, although there is a price guarantee, there is no enforceable guarantee of the quantities that buyers will buy. Fairtrade can fix the price but it cannot fix supply and demand curves and therefore cannot guarantee quantity. In conventional markets, in fact, some commercial buyers of commodities, including transnational firms, do guarantee both prices and quantities through hedging (Russell et al., 2012).

We in no way doubt the value of Fairtrade as a channel for some producers, but it should be understood in context.

Ultimately, the development problem is not a question of whether we can make 10 per cent of smallholders 5 per cent better off through Fairtrade or 30 per cent of smallholders 20 per cent better off through an extension of free trade – or whatever figures we might dispute. Our ancestors were probably smallholders. We became rich not because of a 19th-century version of Fairtrade that kept us in agriculture but because development provided many more employment opportunities enabling the minority who stayed on the land to be far more productive with much more capital equipment. More recently, within a generation, the proportion of people living from the land in South Korea has fallen from over 50 per cent to 7 per cent (Agriculture and Agri-Food Canada, 2009) while output has increased. This is how countries develop given the right environment in terms of good governance, the rule of law, the protection of private property, and the right conditions for business to thrive.

We do not decry the efforts of Fairtrade in trying to improve the lot of producers including some smallholders – the here and now is important. But the question we were asked was about its impact overall compared with conventional trade. The development of conventional trade enables people to produce things that are of much greater value in world markets rather than simply paying people a little more for producing what they were previously producing. It is this which pulls whole nations out of poverty towards prosperity.

Best wishes,
Philip and Sushil

About the authors

Matthew Anderson is a lecturer at Portsmouth Business School, University of Portsmouth, UK.

Philip Booth is Editorial and Programme Director at the Institute of Economic Affairs, London.

Sushil Mohan is Principal Lecturer at University of Brighton.

References

Agriculture and Agri-Food Canada (2009) *South Korea Agriculture Policy Review 2009* [pdf] <http://ageconsearch.umn.edu/bitstream/52051/2/south%20korea_e.pdf> [accessed 1 February 2014].

Chen, S. and Ravallion, M. (2008) 'The developing world is poorer than we thought but no less successful in the fight against poverty', *Policy Research Working Paper 4703, Washington, DC: World Bank.*

Fairtrade International (2012) *Monitoring the scope and benefits of Fairtrade*, 4th edn, Bonn, Germany: FLO.

GlobeScan (2011) 'Shopping Choices Can Make a Positive Difference to Farmers and Workers in Developing Countries: Global Poll' [online] <www.globescan.com/news-and-analysis/press-releases/press-releases-2011/94-press-releases-2011/145-high-trust-and-global-recognition-makes-fairtrade-an-enabler-of-ethical-consumer-choice.html> [accessed 1 February 2014].

International Assessment of Agricultural Science Technology for Development (IAASTD) (2008) *Global Report: Agriculture at a Crossroads*, Washington, DC: Island Press.

Mohan, S. (2010) *Fair Trade Without the Froth*, London: Institute of Economic Affairs.

Nelson, V. and Pound, B. (2009) *The Last Ten Years: A Comprehensive Review of the Literature on the Impact of Fairtrade*, Chatham, UK: Natural Resources Institute, University of Greenwich.

North, M. (2011) 'Banana breakthrough', in J. Bowes (ed.), *The Fairtrade Revolution*, pp. 140–54, London: Pluto Press.

OECD (n.d.) 'Why open markets matter' [website] <www.oecd.org/trade/whyopenmarketsmatter.htm> [accessed 20 January 2014].

Russell, B., Mohan, S. and Banerjee, A. (2012) 'Coffee market liberalisation and the implications for producers in Brazil, Guatemala and India', *The World Bank Economic Review* 26(3): 514–38 <http://dx.doi.org/10.1093/wber/lhr055>.

Traidcraft (2014) 'Fair trade facts' [website] <www.traidcraft.co.uk/news_and_events/press_room/fair_trade_facts> [accessed 1 February 2014].

UNCTAD (2012) *Trade and Development Report, 2012* [pdf] <http://unctad.org/en/Publications Library/tdr2012_en.pdf> [accessed 1 February 2014].

CHAPTER 10

Conclusion: Fairtrade expectations and Fairtrade futures

Valerie Nelson

Abstract

Evaluation approaches need to be updated, to better reflect the nature of the programme or organization being evaluated. Fairtrade has attributes which make it fairly complex. While it has generic standards, its implementation is partly context specific and it is now being implemented in many countries around the globe. It is also a social movement seeking to apply pressure for change both directly with buyers in value chain relationships and indirectly with enabling environment actors. Evaluation approaches need to reflect the broad-ranging scope of sustainability standards such as Fairtrade, and the complexity of the problems which Fairtrade seeks to address. A key starting point is to learn from in-depth case studies as presented in this book and theory-based evaluation approaches which can explore the more immediate contribution of Fairtrade to producer organization survival and development and changes in value chain relationships. Such studies should help to identify strategic changes in approach.

Keywords: context specificity; theory of change; fair sourcing landscapes; systems-based analysis; sustainable landscape initiatives.

Fairtrade cannot be expected to solve rural development challenges on its own. Too often, stakeholder expectations, particularly in consumer countries, have been too high and overly simplistic. Many impact studies focus upon the outcomes and impacts for producers, adopting rigorous experimental methods, but such approaches may not be the most appropriate for evaluating change in complex, adaptive systems – which is what rural landscape economies linked to global value chains essentially are. Tree crops, for example, have very long time-scales for establishment and production and so cycles of expansion and reduction responding to market signals do not necessarily correspond to impact study timetables. Impact studies, even where these are longitudinal multi-year studies, do not have a sufficiently long time-scale to capture differing market conditions. Baselines can be deteriorating where smallholder farmers and communities face increasing market volatility and climatic risks, so support from Fairtrade may be helping to support producers against a worsening background in some cases. Creating robust counterfactual comparisons

http://dx.doi.org/10.3362/9781780449067.010

is very complex given the multiple certifications held by increasing numbers of producer organizations. Some effects could be under-estimated where there is a spillover effect such as raising local market prices for cocoa. Fairtrade is an organization, albeit one with a specific set of generic standards. How it is implemented in a particular place may vary slightly especially where there are different forms of donor or buyer support and engagement. Thus, the intervention has to be unpacked and may be relatively specific to a particular place. For all of these reasons more rigorous experimental evaluation approaches can be very challenging and in some instances may not be the most appropriate.

Using theory-based evaluation is one way of establishing more clearly whether there are plausible effects from an intervention, by unpacking its constituent and combined elements and anticipated impact pathways, and comparing this with evidence on the actual consequences, documenting along the impact pathway. Theory-based evaluation can help to show where there may be weaknesses, as well as strengths, in the Fairtrade approach. In-depth qualitative case studies, as presented in this volume, also help to tease out how Fairtrade is making a contribution (or not) in diverse ways as part of wider processes of social change. The Fairtrade organizational theory of change is, in fact, very wide-ranging with different impact pathways, not all of which have been adequately evaluated. Many studies have focused upon ultimate outcomes and impacts for smallholders and workers, but there has been much less analysis of the impacts of Fairtrade on producer organizations or the contribution of Fairtrade producer networks, changes in value chain relationships achieved by Fairtrade, and global and national advocacy on trade policy and narratives.

In reality, smallholder farmers and disadvantaged workers (formal and informal) in global value chains face many struggles and uncertainties. Being integrated into volatile global commodity markets with weak bargaining power and capacity gaps in organization can be problematic. Producer organizations, such as cooperatives, face major challenges in merely remaining viable businesses in fluctuating global markets and in situations of poor governance, limited access to public services and increasing climate-related risks. In some cases, there is a lack of demand such that the proportion of product sold on Fairtrade terms is limited and this means that the impact of Fairtrade is less likely to be clearly visible to individual members and there is less chance of the producer organization's business becoming a profitable enterprise. Smallholder farmers in some regions of the world face increasing climate-related variability.

Rural development challenges in a particular landscape can be significant, such as weak infrastructure, poor coverage and quality of agricultural advisory services; a democratic deficit in rural governance and insecure land rights; and gender and social inequality. While fairer trading relations in specific value chains could leverage a greater return of resources to producers and provide some level of security net for smallholders in times of low prices, it cannot eliminate market risks, and more importantly, it is hard to see how Fairtrade interventions can overcome such interlocking hurdles on its own. There is thus the need for Fairtrade stakeholders to manage expectations, while also increasing sales – something that is not a straightforward task, particularly as many global companies are beginning to look beyond (or in addition to) certification to own-brand initiatives.

It is also the case that Fairtrade should reflect upon its theory of change. Fairtrade should continue to work to strengthen producer and worker organisation and to push for fairer value chain relations. At the same time, it can innovate in its approach and this could include embracing landscape oriented collaborations. To change a rural economy in a particular place will require systemic change. This means looking beyond the vertical single commodity focus. For some farmers, it may be a good outcome to specialize further in cocoa or coffee production as their producer organization grows stronger, with the support of Fairtrade, but there are risks to this specialization and on a wider landscape level it may not be a good developmental outcome if many farmers specialize further in specific crops which could potentially depress prices. Also where land sizes are diminishing in size and are increasingly fragmented there may be a need for crop diversification and off-farm livelihood opportunities. Engaging with other landscape actors might enable Fairtrade to move beyond this vertical, single-commodity focus. One pathway ahead for Fairtrade could be to explore 'fair sourcing landscapes' or 'fair trade rural economies'. Fairtrade has much in common with the Latin American Rural Territorial Development movement, which focuses upon economic development from a territorial perspective, but includes more awareness of political economy than some current donor-supported landscape initiatives.

There is a move in international development and inclusive business circles towards landscape-oriented initiatives, which, in essence, recognize the limitations of sustainability standards and a focus on individual farms or producer groups, and are shifting to a broader *systems-based* analysis of the rural landscape economy and the multiple value chains that support livelihood systems (both export and domestic). Efforts are being made to identify alternative business models which can increase rewards to producers for sustainable production and land management and protection.

Understanding a rural area landscape from a systems-perspective might provide Fairtrade with new ideas as to how to evolve their approach and who to work with strategically. It is likely that over time Fairtrade may have to move away from the focus on auditing and certification, to more flexible, catalytic and place-based approaches, which stimulate adaptive management of natural resources and are more effective in rewarding producers and communities both for sustainable production and land management.

Fairtrade already includes and supports regional and national producer networks in a bottom-up approach to producer empowerment. It could join the increasing number of multi-stakeholder Sustainable Landscape Initiatives (SLIs) in specific places, sharing their experience and organizational presence, to contribute to systemic change. Fairtrade could help to challenge some of the assumptions regarding the type of value chain relationships which are promoted in such multi-stakeholder processes, encouraging greater consideration of political economy. This is important as, too often, current sector-based multi-stakeholder initiatives are confronting sustainable production issues only from the priorities of industry actors and from a single commodity perspective. Where there are sustainable landscape initiatives, these are recognizing the need for change in the balance of production and protection incentives through the creation of new business models and institutional arrangements, but tend to have a fairly apolitical starting point. This creates the risk that the interests of more powerful actors will be advanced, over and above those with lesser voice. By supporting producers' voice in such processes, Fairtrade could play an important role in facilitating a return of power to the local via fairer trading relations in diverse commodities.

The composition of 'producer voice' should be unpacked. Who in the rural landscape is being empowered to have a voice? Enabling smallholders to have a greater voice in future rural development is critically important, but so too is the wider community including informal workers, for example. Embracing wider landscape approaches may provide Fairtrade with a clearer vision of the differences between rural dwellers, acting upon gender and labour relations more effectively. Similarly, Fairtrade could engage citizens (not just consumers) in advocacy on fairer trade, creating alliances across scale. Civic innovation requires bottom-up approaches, but also cross-scale alliances.

In sum, rural development challenges are highly complex, requiring simultaneous change from multiple actors. Highly complex or 'wicked' problems, such as poverty, environmental degradation, adapting to climate change, and unfair trade, involve multiple organizations and have diverse and unclear causes and solutions. System change requires changing mindsets and narratives, such that there are combined changes in the practices of different actors and organizations. For Fairtrade, this means changes amongst value chain actors, but also amongst wider landscape actors, including government at national and sub-regional levels. Fairtrade cannot solve highly complex problems alone, but it can make a positive and important contribution, particularly if it can move beyond the vertical, single commodity focus, embodied in the auditing and certification approach, and engage with wider rural realities. Fairtrade could participate in and support a shift to systems-thinking in rural economic development, promoting a stronger awareness of *political economy* issues in vertical value chain initiatives and in horizontal governance and multi-stakeholder landscape initiatives. Fairtrade has a key role in facilitating bottom-up producer, worker and community movements anchored in specific landscapes or territories and connecting these to activists and consumers elsewhere.

A key element of rural economic development and a response to growing and urgent sustainability challenges is working out the kind of rural futures that are desired in particular places. This includes the visions and imaginaries of smallholders and community level actors, which may otherwise be side-lined in multi-stakeholder landscape or value chain initiatives. There is an opportunity for Fairtrade to contribute to supporting local voices, particularly women and marginalized groups, in this articulation process (not necessarily leading it). Fairtrade has to work strategically with key partners to challenge inequitable trading relations and to scale up change in specific territories. The difference between Fairtrade and an international development NGO lies in its experience and engagement with international activists, consumers and buyers (corporate-, mission- or speciality-driven). It can seek to work at the intersection of global value chains, which hold the potential to return capital to the small producers and workers for sustainable production through fairer and more supportive trading relationships, with wider landscape processes of rural development. This may require further development of the theory of change and a review of current organizational structure and approaches to support more flexible, systems-based interventions and civic grassroots innovations.

About the author

Valerie Nelson is Principal Scientist, Social Development Specialist and Reader in International Development at the Natural Resources Institute (NRI), University of Greenwich, UK. She leads the Equitable Trade and Responsible Business Programme at the NRI.